Ready for
PET

Nick Kenny   Anne Kelly

MACMILLAN
HEINEMANN
English Language Teaching

Macmillan Heinemann English Language Teaching
Between Towns Road, Oxford OX4 3PP
A division of Macmillan Publishers Limited
Companies and representatives throughout the world

ISBN 0 333 93393 1 (without Key)
      0 333 93392 3 (with Key)

Text © Nick Kenny and Anne Kelly
Design and illustration © Macmillan Publishers Limited 2001
Heinemann is a registered trademark of Reed Educational and Professional Publishing Limited

First published 2001

Designed by Jim Evoy
Illustrated by Mike Atkinson and David Smith
Cover idea by Xen Media Ltd

The authors would like to thank Barbara Lewis in Pescara, Italy, for
her help with this book.

The publishers would like to thank the following consultants and
teachers for piloting and reviewing this book: Andy Hannaford,
Anthony Matthews, Barbara Lewis, Gail Butler, Mabel Turner and
Sarah Ellis.

The authors and publishers would like to thank the following for
permission to reproduce copyright material: University of
Cambridge Local Examinations Syndicate – EFL for the answer
sheets on pp.92–3.

LONDON METRO, for 'New Boy at University is Just Six', published
in Metro, 16 February 2000.

TIME OUT, for 'A Brood Awakening', published in Time Out No.
1563, 2-9 August 2000.

The authors and publishers would like to thank the following for
permission to reproduce their photographs: Sue Baker © MHELT
p18(br); Corbis pp21, 27, Corbis / Stephanie Colasanti 51, Corbis /
Michael Dunn 25(tr), Corbis / David Giles 25(tl), Corbis / Philip Gould
47(m), Corbis / Robert Holmes 38, Corbis / David Turnley 47(b), Corbis
/ Wartenberg 28, Corbis / Wartenberg 60, Corbis / David Wells 63(m);
Haddon Davies © MHELT pp8 (tmr), 16 (3, 4), 54(5); English Heritage
Photo Library p31; Eye Ubiquitous pp91(b), Eye Ubiquitous / Tim
Hawkins 48(m), Eye Ubiquitous / Craig Hutchins pp39, Eye
Ubiquitous / Craig Hutchins 41(b), Eye Ubiquitous / Craig Hutchins
48(ml), Eye Ubiquitous / Julia Waterlow 48(mr); Chris Honeywell ©
MHELT p18(mr); Image Bank pp43, 78(t), 91; MHELT pp8 (l, ml, m, r),
16 (1, 4, 5), 54(1, 2, 3, 4), 56 (2, 3, 4); Photodisc pp56 (1, 2);Pictor
p63(b); Stone pp19, 33, 41(t), 78(b), 42; Sunday Times (Funday Times)
p44; Telegraph Colour Library pp6, 12(tr); John Walmsley p12(tl).

Printed and bound in Spain by
Mateu Cromo

2005 2004 2003 2002 2001
10 9 8 7 6 5 4 3 2 1

Contents

Introduction

	What is the Preliminary English Test (PET)?	2
	How *Ready for PET* is organized	3
	For students studying alone	4
	PET preparation diary	5

Unit 1 Lesson 1: Personal information — 6
Lesson 2: A regular thing — 9

Unit 2 Lesson 1: You live and learn — 12
Lesson 2: All the best books — 15

Unit 3 Lesson 1: Holiday adventures — 18
Lesson 2: Just the job — 21

Unit 4 Lesson 1: House and home — 24
Lesson 2: Interesting people — 27

Unit 5 Lesson 1: Places of interest — 30
Lesson 2: Getting there — 33

Unit 6 Lesson 1: What a bargain! — 36
Lesson 2: City life — 39

Unit 7 Lesson 1: Food and drink — 42
Lesson 2: Your own space — 45

Unit 8 Lesson 1: Close to nature — 48
Lesson 2: The wide world — 51

Unit 9 Lesson 1: Free time — 54
Lesson 2: Get well soon! — 57

Unit 10 Lesson 1: Entertainment — 60
Lesson 2: The age of communication — 63

Practice Test 1

Reading Part 1	66
Reading Part 2	67
Reading Part 3	68
Reading Part 4	69
Reading Part 5	70
Writing Part 1	71
Writing Part 2	71
Writing Part 3	72
Listening Part 1	73
Listening Part 2	74
Listening Part 3	74
Listening Part 4	75
Speaking	76–78

Practice Test 2

Reading Part 1	79
Reading Part 2	80
Reading Part 3	81
Reading Part 4	82
Reading Part 5	83
Writing Part 1	84
Writing Part 2	84
Writing Part 3	85
Listening Part 1	86
Listening Part 2	87
Listening Part 3	87
Listening Part 4	88
Speaking	89–91

Answer sheets — 92–93

Irregular verbs — 94

Introduction

Ready for PET is for students of English who are preparing to take the University of Cambridge Preliminary English Test (PET). *Ready for PET* will get you ready for this test in three important ways. First, it will give you practice in doing the kinds of exercises you will do in the test. Then, it will give you advice on how you can do your best in these exercises. Finally, it will help you learn the vocabulary you need to do the writing and speaking exercises fluently. In this way, you can feel confident about your English when you do the test.

You can use *Ready for PET* in your English class with your teacher, or you can use it to get ready for the test by yourself.

What is the Preliminary English Test (PET)?

The University of Cambridge has tests for students of English at five different levels, from beginners to very advanced students.

PET is at level 2 and is for lower intermediate students. PET tests your reading, writing, listening and speaking. You get 25% of the total marks for the test for each of these four skills. There are three different papers.

Paper 1 is Reading and Writing and takes 1 hour and 30 minutes. In this paper, there are five reading parts and three writing parts. In the reading part of the paper, you have to read some texts and answer some questions on each one. For these questions, you answer by choosing A, B, C, or D. In the writing part of the paper, you have to do a short grammar exercise, fill in a form and then write a letter. This is a summary of the Reading and Writing paper:

Paper 1: Reading and Writing (1 hour 30 minutes)			
	Type of text	**Type of question**	**Number of questions and marks**
Reading			
Part 1	five signs or notices	reading comprehension: multiple choice	5
Part 2	eight short texts	reading comprehension: matching	5
Part 3	one text	reading comprehension: correct/not correct	10
Part 4	one text	reading comprehension: multiple choice	5
Part 5	one text	vocabulary and grammar: multiple choice	10
Writing			
Part 1		grammar	5
Part 2		filling in a form	10
Part 3		writing a letter	10

Paper 2 is Listening and takes about 30 minutes. There are four parts to the paper. You have to listen to a recording and answer some questions. For the questions for three parts, you answer by choosing A, B, C, or D, and for one part you write down a few words or numbers. You hear each part of the recording twice. This is a summary of the Listening paper:

	Paper 2: Listening (approximately 30 minutes)		
	Type of text	Type of question	Number of questions and marks
Part 1	seven short recordings (one or two people speaking)	multiple choice pictures	7
Part 2	one person speaking	multiple choice	6
Part 3	one person speaking	writing down words	6
Part 4	two people speaking	correct/not correct	6

Paper 3 is Speaking and takes 10–12 minutes. There are four parts to the paper. You do the Speaking test with another student. In the Speaking test, you and your partner talk to an examiner and to each other, while another examiner listens to you. The examiner will ask you some questions and give you some instructions about what you should talk about. In two parts, you have some pictures to talk about. This is a summary of the Speaking paper:

	Paper 3: Speaking (10–12 minutes)
Part 1	You and your partner ask and answer questions about yourselves.
Part 2	You and your partner look at some pictures showing a situation and talk about it together.
Part 3	You and your partner take it in turns to describe a photograph each.
Part 4	You and your partner have a conversation about the subject (eg holidays) of your photos.

You will find more detailed information about each part of all three papers in the different lessons of *Ready for PET*.

How Ready for PET is organized

There are ten units in *Ready for PET* and each unit has two lessons. In each unit, you will find exercises to practise the reading, writing, listening and speaking skills, and the vocabulary and grammar you will need in PET. In each lesson of Units 1–8, there is detailed information and advice about one particular part of the test, and in Units 9–10 you can revise all the advice that has gone before. Throughout the book there are **Get ready** boxes containing clear, helpful exam tips.

At the end of the book there are two PET practice tests. When you do these, you will experience what it is like taking the real test. You will see how much time you have to do each question and you will find out which parts of the test you need to practise more.

When you've worked through *Ready for PET*, you'll know what to expect in every part of the test, and you'll have the language you need to do the test well.

For students studying alone

If you are preparing for PET without a teacher, *Ready for PET* will help you. You should use *Ready for PET* at the same time as your general English coursebook. Your coursebook will develop your knowledge of English, and *Ready for PET* will give you the special practice you need for the test exercises.

There is a special 'with key' edition of *Ready for PET* which has a key to exercises and tapescripts of the listening texts at the back. When you have finished each exercise, check your answers with the key. Don't look at the key until you have done each exercise. If necessary, you can use a dictionary to help you with unknown words, but always try to guess the meaning of words first. You should also see if you can answer the questions without knowing the difficult words.

The texts of the listening exercises are on cassette. In the PET Listening test, you hear each listening text twice, so when you are practising with these exercises, rewind the tape and listen again before checking your answers. If you don't understand something you can look at the tapescript, but never do this until you have listened to the tape twice.

There are many writing exercises in *Ready for PET*. It's useful if you can ask a teacher to correct these for you, but it doesn't matter if this isn't possible. Just doing the writing is good practice. Always make sure you follow the instructions exactly and check your own work carefully.

There are also many speaking exercises in the book. It's difficult to do speaking exercises if you're studying alone, but it's important that you get speaking practice. Remember, 25% of the marks for the whole of PET are for the Speaking test, so if possible, do the speaking exercises with another student. If you can't do this, do the exercises by yourself, speaking into a cassette recorder. Then listen to yourself speaking and think of ways in which you could do the exercise better. Don't worry about making mistakes, but try to express your ideas clearly.

On pages 66–91, there are two practice tests. You should try to do at least one of these like a real test. Only take the amount of time allowed for the test, and do it without any dictionary or notes to help you.

Before you start, decide how many hours a week you can spend studying with *Ready for PET* and keep to this decision. It is better to study regularly for short periods than to try and do everything just before the day of the test.

The PET preparation diary on the opposite page will help you to organize your study. Fill in the date you start your PET preparation at the top, and the date you will take PET at the bottom. Then work out how many days or weeks you have to complete each unit of this book. When you have completed a unit, write the date in the space provided, and decide how well you have done in the different practice exercises in that unit (self-assessment). In the 'Study notes' section you can write anything which will help you. For example, you may want to make a note of some exercises you want to look at again, or some exercises which you haven't had time to do and plan to work on later. You should organize your study in the way which best suits you in the time you have available before you take PET.

PET preparation diary

I began preparing for PET on: (date) ....

Unit	Study notes	Self-assessment ✔ = I did well ✘ = I need more practice
1 completed on		Reading Listening Speaking Writing Vocabulary Grammar
2 completed on		Reading Listening Speaking Writing Vocabulary Grammar
3 completed on		Reading Listening Speaking Vocabulary Grammar
4 completed on		Reading Listening Speaking Writing Vocabulary Grammar
5 completed on		Reading Listening Speaking Writing Vocabulary
6 completed on		Reading Listening Speaking Writing Vocabulary
7 completed on		Reading Listening Speaking Vocabulary Grammar
8 completed on		Reading Listening Speaking Vocabulary Grammar
9 completed on		Reading Speaking Writing Vocabulary Grammar
10 completed on		Reading Listening Speaking Writing Vocabulary Grammar

I am taking PET on: (test date) ....

1 ① Personal information

1 Writing Complete this form with information about yourself.

PERSONAL FACTFILE

Name: ....

Surname: ....

Address: ....

....

Sex: ....

Age: ....

Occupation: ....

Interests: ....

....

....

....

---

2 Listening 🔊 1 Listen to two people talking about themselves and complete their personal factfiles.

PERSONAL FACTFILE

Name: ....

Surname: ....

Address: ....

....

Sex: ....

Age: ....

Occupation: ....

Interests: ....

....

....

....

A

PERSONAL FACTFILE

Name: ....

Surname: ....

Address: ....

....

Sex: ....

Age: ....

Occupation: ....

Interests: ....

....

....

....

B

2 If you wanted to find out more information about these people, what questions would you ask? Make questions beginning with each of these words.

Are... ?

What... ?

When... ?

Do... ?

How... ?

Where... ?

3 Speaking

1 Look at the activities in the box. Which of these activities are you good at? Order the activities from most interesting (1) to least interesting (12).

Talk about why you like (1) and why you dislike (12).

watching sports	playing sports	computer games
watersports	collecting things	playing a musical instrument
dancing	learning languages	making things
driving	keep-fit exercises	surfing the Internet

2 David and Victoria have just met at a party. Complete the gaps in their conversation using the phrases below. Write the correct letters in the spaces.

David: Hello. I'm David.
Victoria: **(1)** ....
David: Yes, I'm one of his friends too, and we play football together. What do you study?
Victoria: **(2)** ....
David: I've finished college, actually, and I'm working as a windsurfing instructor.
Victoria: **(3)** ....
David: That doesn't matter. You could learn.
Victoria: **(4)** ....
David: So am I. I'm running a course which starts next week. Would you be interested in joining?
Victoria: **(5)** ....

Use five of these phrases to complete Victoria's part of the conversation.

A English. Have you finished college?
B Yes, I suppose so. But what I'm really interested in is sailing.
C Hi. I'm Victoria. I'm a friend of Tom's from college.
D Hello, I'm Victoria. I'm really interested in football.
E I'm doing languages. What about you?
F Oh, I'm really interested in watersports, but I'm not very good at windsurfing.
G Oh... I might be... it depends.

3 Which two didn't you use? Now listen and check.

4 When you meet someone of your own age for the first time:
- what questions do you ask them?
- what are good things to talk about?
- what do you tell them about yourself?

4 Writing

You have decided to join an English-language club on the Internet. Write a brief description of yourself for the database. You can write up to 100 words. Remember to include:
- your personal details, for example, name and age
- what you do/study
- the things that you are interested in

5 Listening 😀 Listen to these people giving personal information. As you listen, make a note of their names, addresses and telephone numbers.

Person	Name	Address	Telephone number
1			
2			
3			
4			
5			

6 Grammar Finish the second sentence so that it means the same as the first.

1 Do you play football well?
  Are you... *plaing football well ?*
2 Do watersports interest you?
  Are you... *intersting watersport*
3 What is your age?
  How ... *old are you*
4 Where exactly do you live?
  What is... *your address*
5 How is your surname spelt?
  How do you ... *speling you surname*

7 Reading 1 Look at these notices and choose the correct explanation, A, B, C, or D.

Notice 1 is telling you:
A where to write.
B what to write about.
C which type of letters to use.
D which type of pen to use.

1
> Please write in
> **BLOCK CAPITALS**

Notice 2 is giving you:
A some advice.
B a suggestion.
C an instruction.
D a warning.

2
> **ALL PACKAGES
> MUST BE
> SIGNED FOR**

2 What is a signature? How is it different from other ways of writing your name?
Write your name in block capitals: *I. IVANOV*
Write your signature: *(signature)*

A regular thing

1 Match the words in A with the words in B. For example, *comb* and *hair* go together. Some words are used more than once.

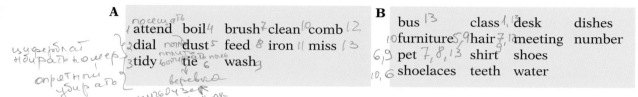

A

attend boil brush clean comb
dial dust feed iron miss
tidy tie wash

B

bus   class desk   dishes
furniture hair meeting number
pet shirt shoes
shoelaces teeth water

Which of these things do you do regularly, sometimes, occasionally, or never? Talk about some of your habits using the words in the boxes.

2 Now match the words in C with the words in D. Some words are used more than once.

C

hand in	join in	take off
put on	put up	put away
turn up	plug in	turn on

D

books	game	homework
make-up	music	radio
socks	umbrella	light

Use the words in the boxes to talk about your daily life.

Do you like listening to the radio? Why? Why not?
- An international radio station wants to find out about its listeners.
- You have agreed to complete a questionnaire for the radio station.
- Look at the questionnaire and answer each question.

Radio Good Times
22 Coast Road,
Brighton BN21 5AH, UK

Please tell us about yourself:

Full name: **(1)** ....

Home address: **(2)** ....

Nationality: **(3)** ....

Date of birth (day/month/year): **(4)**..

Occupation: **(5)**...

How many hours a week do you listen to the radio? **(6)** ....

What type of radio programme do you listen to most? **(7)**....................................

Where do you listen to the radio? **(8)** ....

What activities do you do while listening? **(9)** ....

Which famous English-speaking person would you like us to interview on the radio? **(10)**...

Thank you for answering our questions!

Get ready for PET Writing Part 2

1 You should complete the questionnaire giving real information about yourself. However, if you never listen to the radio, imagine that you do and invent answers to questions 6–10.
2 Write about one to four words (or figures) in each space.
3 For question 2, don't forget to include the name of your country.

4 For question 3, if, for example, you come from Spain, your nationality is Spanish. If you come from Brazil, your nationality is Brazilian. Make sure you spell your nationality correctly and use a capital letter.
5 For question 5, write what you do. For example, *student*, *accountant*, or *unemployed*.
6 Look at the questionnaire below. None of the answers is satisfactory. Why not?

Radio Good Times
22 Coast Road,
Brighton BN21 5AH, UK

Please tell us about yourself:

Full name: **(1)** .... *Ralf* ....
Home address: **(2)** .... *Berlin* ....
Nationality: **(3)** .... *Germany* ....
Date of birth (day/month/year): **(4)** .... *july 1987* ....
Occupation: **(5)** .... *school* ....
How many hours a week do you listen to the radio? **(6)** .... *200* ....
What type of radio programme do you listen to most? **(7)** .... *TV* ....
Where do you listen to the radio? **(8)** .... *no* ....
What activities do you do while listening? **(9)** .... *car* ....
Which famous English-speaking person would you like us to interview on the radio? **(10)** .... *Napoleon Bonaparte* ....

Thank you for answering our questions!

---

3 Grammar

There are several ways to make comparisons.
Examples:
*Sam listens to the radio **more** often **than** Marcia does.*
*Marcia listens to the radio **less** often **than** Sam does.*
*Marcia doesn't listen to the radio **as** often **as** Sam does.*

*My shoes are clean**er than** my brother's.*
*My brother's shoes are dirt**ier than** mine.*
*My brother's shoes aren't **as** clean **as** mine.*

*My grandmother is **better** at ironing **than** my mother.*
*My mother is not **as** good at ironing **as** my grandmother.*
*My mother is **worse** at ironing **than** my grandmother.*

Finish the second sentence so that it means the same as the first.

1 Your bedroom is tidier than mine.
   My bedroom isn't ....

2 Gerry doesn't do the washing-up as fast as Paul.
   Paul does the washing-up ....

3 The new armchair isn't nearly as comfortable as the old one.
   The old armchair is much ....

4 Every evening, Sally does a lot more homework than Rachel.
   Every evening, Rachel does a lot ....

5 This music isn't nearly as bad as the music they play on Radio 2.
   The music they play on Radio 2 is far ....

4 Reading

1 **What inventions of the last 2,000 years have caused the most important changes in people's daily lives?**

2 **Read this text and choose the correct word, A, B, C or D for each space.**

INVENTIONS OF THE LAST 2,000 YEARS

Recently, hundreds of scientists and philosophers were asked to name the most important invention of the last 2,000 years. You might **(1)**............ people to say the Internet, penicillin or the internal combustion engine, but in **(2)**............ nobody did. One scientist **(3)**............ for paper because, long before the Internet, paper allowed ideas to be sent around the world. **(4)**............ scientists agreed that modern medicine has helped millions of people, but said **(5)**............ inventions, such as soap and pipes for clean and dirty water, have **(6)**............ more lives. One philosopher said hay was the most important because it's winter food for horses. Without **(7)**............ , horses couldn't exist in cold climates, **(8)**............ meant that there couldn't be cities in places colder than Athens and Rome. So, thanks **(9)**............ hay, Vienna, Paris, London and Berlin were built! Someone else named the mirror because in **(10)**............ at our own faces we can learn about human beings in general.

1	**A** expect	**B** think	**C** believe	**D** guess
2	**A** all	**B** fact	**C** particular	**D** detail
3	**A** suggested	**B** judged	**C** answered	**D** voted
4	**A** Other	**B** Another	**C** Others	**D** Any
5	**A** clearer	**B** plainer	**C** simpler	**D** purer
6	**A** rescued	**B** delivered	**C** saved	**D** recovered
7	**A** them	**B** it	**C** these	**D** many
8	**A** what	**B** that	**C** where	**D** which
9	**A** to	**B** of	**C** by	**D** from
10	**A** seeing	**B** looking	**C** watching	**D** studying

2 You live and learn

1 Vocabulary

1 Look at the photographs.

A

B

In which of the photos can you see these things?

mouse	screen	desk
blackboard	keyboard	pen
chair	map	

somebody...
asking	thinking
talking	reading
explaining	waiting

2 What other things can you see in the photographs?

2 Speaking

1 Look at these ideas. Which five do you think are the best ways to learn English?

surfing the Internet
studying a textbook
going to classes
playing computer games
doing grammar exercises

?

listening to songs
watching satellite TV
talking to people in English
watching films in English
reading newspapers and magazines

2 Listen to Polly. She is studying Spanish.

- Which is her favourite way of studying Spanish?
- Choose the correct picture.

 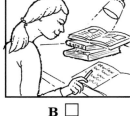  

A ☐　　　　　B ☐　　　　　C ☐　　　　　D ☐

- Why does Polly like studying in this way?

3 You want to ask Polly about the things in the box below. Write the questions.

the teacher	length of each class	number of students
the book(s) and equipment	type of people	cost of course
the classroom	number of classes per week	what she's learnt

Get ready for PET Speaking Part 1

1 In the exam you have to *talk to your partner*.
2 Before the exam, you need lots of practice in *asking* questions correctly.
3 When you *answer* questions, say what you think and explain why.

4 Make the conversation *interesting*, add extra information, ask questions, and react to what your partner says.

3 Speaking

1 **Look at this situation.**

A young friend of yours wants to learn a new language in his free time.
He has a small amount of money to spend on this new hobby.
First, talk about the things he can buy to help him learn the language.
Then, say which will be the best use of his money.

Get ready for PET Speaking Part 2

1 Listen to the instructions. Are you talking about yourself or somebody else?
2 Speak to your partner, not to the examiner.
3 Remember to *listen* to your partner and *respond* to what (s)he says.
4 Say *what* you think and explain *why* you think it.

Examples:
I think x is a good idea because...
I think x is better than y because...
I think (s)he should buy x because...
I think the best thing (for him/her) to buy is x because...

2 Pietro and Valerie are doing exercise 3.1. Complete the gaps in their conversation using the phrases below. Write the correct letters in the spaces.

Valerie: So, our friend wants to learn a new language?
Pietro: **(1)** ....
Valerie: No, he can't. Let's start by talking about which of them will be useful for him.
Pietro: **(2)** ....
Valerie: OK. Shall we start with this one, the dictionary?
Pietro: **(3)** ....
Valerie: Yes, I agree, and it's also good for checking spelling. But what about a textbook? They're useful too.
Pietro: **(4)** ....
Valerie: Possibly. Or he may get one free when he pays for the course.
Pietro: **(5)** ....

Use five of these phrases to complete Pietro's part of the conversation.

A Oh yes, that's a good point.
B I don't like them very much.
C Yes they are, but maybe he won't need one because he'll have a teacher.
D Would you like a dictionary or a textbook?
E OK, then afterwards we can decide which one he should buy.
F That's right, and he's only got £20 to spend, so he can't buy all these things, can he?
G Yes, I think he should buy one of those, because it's very useful if you don't know what words mean.

3 Which two phrases didn't you use? Now listen and check.

4 Listening

- Look at these five statements.
- Listen to Tim and Janet talking about the courses they are doing in their free time.
- Decide if each statement is correct or incorrect.
- If you think it is correct, put a tick (✓) in the box under **A** for **Yes**. If you think it is not correct, put a tick (✓) in the box under **B** for **No**.

		A Yes	B No
1	Janet thinks her computer classes are too long.	☐	☐
2	Tim has learnt many new things on his course.	☐	☐
3	Tim has to buy the food he cooks on his course.	☐	☐
4	Tim asks Janet to help him with his cookery.	☐	☐
5	Janet agrees to help Tim solve a problem.	☐	☐

5 Grammar

Finish the second sentence so that it means the same as the first.
1 Each lesson is two hours long.
Each lesson lasts ....
2 What's the price of this CD ROM, please?
How ....
3 I think a dictionary is very useful.
In my ....
4 I think that you are right about the textbook.
I agree ....
5 What about talking about the videotape first?
Let's ....

All the best books

1 Reading

Read the notices and answer the questions.
- Which one can you probably see in **a)** a library? **b)** a bookshop?
- Which one is **a)** advertising something? **b)** warning you?
- What does each notice mean? Choose **A**, **B**, **C** or **D**.

1

Just published -

Mediterranean Cookery
by **Poppy Tobin**

Signed copies available on request

A We have published all of Poppy Tobin's books about cooking.
B Watch someone give a cooking demonstration here today.
C Sign here if you'd like a copy of Poppy Tobin's latest book.
D Buy a new book with the writer's signature in it here.

2

Please respect all books in your care.

Heavy fines for any damage to borrowed books.

A Take care when looking at damaged books.
B You'll have to pay if you don't look after our books.
C It's fine to borrow these books except for the heavy ones.
D You can use these books here, but you can't borrow them.

2 Vocabulary

Look at these book covers. What type of book do you think each one is? Choose your answers from the words in the box.

mystery	romance	horror	science fiction
thriller	biography	humour	travel

Which of these books would you like to read? Why do you enjoy this type of book?

A
B
C
D
E
F
G
H

3 Reading

The people in 1–5 all want to buy a book.
- Look at the descriptions of eight books (A–H).
- Decide which one would be most suitable for each person.

1 Laura is looking for a book for her grandson's fifth birthday present. Preferably, it should be about space travel or animals and be a story she can read to him many times.

2 Moira's 14-year-old daughter loves science fiction videos. Moira wants to encourage her to read more by giving her a book which will hold her attention.

3 Fiona, like everyone in her family, is very interested in the cinema and enjoys reading about it. She wants a book that will give her all the gossip about film stars past and present.

4 James, who is 15, is looking for something to pass the time on a long plane journey. He'd like to read an adventure story which brings a period of history to life.

5 Gerry likes mystery stories which are full of suspense and excitement. He'd prefer to buy a book by a new writer.

This week's bargain books

A The Meeting
This exciting novel is aimed at teenagers but adults will enjoy it, too. It's the 16th century and Per, the farm boy, rescues a princess. There are marvellous chases, battle scenes and romantic meetings – you couldn't ask for more thrilling action in a story, or a more realistic picture of the past.

B Stealing Scenes
Starting at the age of five, the writer of this amusing autobiography has had a long and successful career as an actress on stage and screen. She takes us into her world of lights and cameras and tells the secrets of famous people she has known.

C The Bucketful of Dinosaurs
When Harry finds a bucketful of dinosaurs, he's delighted and takes them everywhere he goes until one day he leaves them on a train. How will he prove that the dinosaurs belong to him? Very young children will never get tired of listening to this charming adventure.

D Blood Rain
In this seventh book in the series about an Italian police inspector, the hero investigates a murder. The victim? Maybe just a friendless nobody, or perhaps the son of the country's most powerful criminal. Can the inspector manage both to find the murderer and to stay alive?

E Hex Shadows
This story is set in the year 2367 when Britain is a part of the cruel European Federation. Hexes, human computers who were created in the late 21st century, are now hunted down as enemies of the Federation. This is an exciting, fast-moving story which teenagers will love.

F Space Age
Designed with the fact-hungry child in mind, this gives information about stars, galaxies, astronauts and spaceships. It will bring the universe to life and make science and technology fun for those between five and ten years old.

G Stormy Weather
This thriller is the first from the pen of a young Canadian. It follows the story of Dale, a meteorologist who is invited on a small plane to watch a thunderstorm. Dale soon discovers that not all dangers come from nature, and to save his life he must find the answers to some deadly questions.

H Shoot!
For more than 20 years, this has been recognized as the best guide to the movies. This latest edition gives details and opinions about more than 22,000 films. It tells you about video availability, which films are suitable for family viewing, and the prizes films have won.

Get ready for PET Reading Part 2

1 Look at the information about Laura. Underline the words that are important about her.
Have you underlined: *grandson's fifth birthday, space travel or animals* and *read... many times*?

2 Which book would be suitable for a child of five (*grandson's fifth birthday*)? Are A, B or E suitable? Why not?
What about C and F? Why? (*very young children, those between five and ten years old*)

3 Are C and F about *space travel* or *animals*? Remember, dinosaurs are animals.

4 C and F can't both be suitable. Which one is unsuitable? Why? So which is the most suitable book for Laura?

5 Now do the same for the other people.

4 Vocabulary

Harry had a *bucketful* of dinosaurs. Complete these sentences in an interesting way.

1 Brian can't speak because he's just taken a mouthful of ....

2 You won't get better unless you swallow this spoonful of ....

3 When nobody was looking, Katia gave me a handful of ....

4 Graham felt hungry when he looked at the plateful of ....

5 Jenny's jacket was heavy because she had a pocketful of ....

5 Writing

Write this letter:

• You have an English friend called Lucy.
• Last week, Lucy lent you her favourite book, but while you had the book it was damaged.
• Now you want to write a short letter to Lucy about the damaged book.
• In your letter, apologize for the damage, explain how it happened, and offer to do something about it. Write about 100 words.

> *Dear Lucy,*
> *Something terrible has happened.* ....
> ....

Here are some useful phrases that you can use in your writing.

To apologize to someone, you can write:

> *I'm very sorry I didn't look after your book very well.*
> *Please forgive me.*

To explain the order in which something happened, you can write:

> *First (this happened), next (that happened), then (something else happened), and finally (this happened).*

To offer to do something for someone, you can write:

> *I'll buy you a new one.*
> *I can mend it for you.*
> *If you like, I'll give you mine.*
> *Let me help you.*

3 ① Holiday adventures

**Read these notices. Which one can you see a) in a travel agency window?
b) at an airport? c) in a hotel?**

1

Find out about
excursions, nightlife
and transport to the
airport at our 24-hour
reception desk

2

70,000 package holidays
Reservations 9 am - 6 pm

Leave an answerphone
message outside
these hours

3

Do not leave
your luggage
unattended
at any time

What does each notice mean? Choose A, B, C or D.

A Make sure there's always someone with your belongings.
B Ask the receptionist if you want your suitcases carried downstairs.
C You can make a booking here during the day.
D Someone is always available to give you information.

**1 Look at picture A and answer these
questions. Use the words in the box.**
1 Who can you see in the picture?
2 Where is she?
3 What's she doing?
4 What things can you see in the picture?
5 How does the girl probably feel? Why?

suitcase	young	wearing	packing
bedroom	nervous	clothes	holiday
quilt	abroad	plastic	woman

A

2 Now use your answers to describe the picture.
Begin: *This picture shows a young woman in her bedroom. She's ...*

**3 Now look at picture B. Describe what
you can see in the picture. Talk about:**
- where the picture was taken
- the people
- what they are doing
- the things you can see
- what they are probably talking about

Use these words:

jacket	phone	writing
curly	arrangements	brochures
discussing	travel agency	shelf
desk	trip	pen

B

Begin: *This picture shows two people in a travel agency. They're ...*

3 Reading

1 How many of these questions do you answer with 'Yes'?

- Are you interested in wildlife and beautiful scenery?
- Do you enjoy camping?
- Do you prefer to go on holiday with a large group of people?
- Would you like to travel in foreign countries?

If you've answered 'Yes' four times, then you'd probably like the kind of holiday shown below. Do you agree? Why or why not?

2 Read the text to decide if each statement is correct or incorrect.

1 In a safari truck, passengers take it in turns to sit next to a window.
2 Safari trucks are able to travel over all types of roads.
3 Safari team leaders have a minimum of 12 months' touring experience.
4 The second driver is as experienced as the team leader.
5 Each truck comes supplied with all the food needed for the trip.
6 Everyone is expected to help get meals ready.
7 What people pay for their food depends on how much they eat.
8 There is always enough clean drinking water.
9 Campers have plenty of space in their tents.
10 Hot showers are provided for campers wherever they stop for the night.

Safari Holidays

If you want to get really close to the wildlife and scenery of Africa, then a Safari Holiday offers the most excitement and best value for money.

The Right Trucks for Africa

Each of our safari trucks is a safe, reliable vehicle which is suited to African travel conditions and allows you to fully enjoy the areas visited. Every seat is a window seat and the sides of the truck can be rolled up to provide a wide space for looking out. We use four-wheel-drive vehicles because roads can be rough or get washed away, and we don't want to be prevented from visiting interesting areas.

The Safari Team

Three of our employees go on each safari trip, one of whom is the team leader. All safari team leaders are fully trained and have worked for at least a year on a wide variety of trips in Africa before they lead their first safari. The team leader is a driver, mechanic, guide, diplomat and general expert on Africa. He is helped by a second driver, usually a team leader in training. The third member of the team, the cook, is as important as the leader. He or she sees that all cooking and camp tasks are completed as smoothly as possible.

Good Food

Safari Holidays are famous for their open-fire cooking. We stop regularly to buy fresh fruit, vegetables and meat in local markets and we also have a good supply of things like tea, coffee, dried milk and tinned food in the truck. All the members of the tour lend a hand with the food preparation and washing-up, under the experienced eye of the team cook. At the beginning of each trip, everyone, including the safari team members, pays the same amount of money into the safari purse and this covers food expenses. All water carried on the truck is safe to drink and we make sure it never runs out.

Quality Camping Equipment

Each truck carries everything needed for the trip. This includes four-person tents, used for only two people, air beds, mosquito nets, camp chairs, a fire grill for campfire cooking and all necessary cooking equipment, a cool box for storing fresh food, binoculars, books on Africa and a first-aid kit.

Accommodation

On Safari Holidays, we sometimes camp in an official campsite and sometimes we put up our tents in wild areas. Some campsites have very basic or no facilities, while at others hot showers and cold drinks are available. At the start or finish of tours, we usually have a night in a hotel. These are clean, comfortable and reasonably priced.

1 Don't worry about the meaning of every word. You don't have to understand every word in the text, only the ones which help you do the task.

2 Use the headings to help you find the answers. In which paragraphs can you find the answers to statements 4, 6, and 9?

3 Underline the words in the text which help you with each statement. What words will you underline for statements 1, 3, and 8?

4 Decide if the words in the text and the statement have the same meaning. Look at number 1. Does *Passengers take it in turns to sit next to a window* mean the same as *Every seat is a window seat*? What about number 2? Does the statement mean the same as the sentence which begins *We use four-wheel-drive vehicles...* ?

---

4 Grammar

There are several ways to say *when* something happens.
Examples:
*Safari drivers must work for a year **before** they can become team leaders.*
*Safari drivers can become team leaders **after** they have worked for a year.*
*Safari drivers can't become team leaders **until** they have worked for a year.*

***When** the campers have put up their tents, they start cooking dinner.*
*The campers start cooking dinner **as soon as** they have put up their tents.*

*Safari members make a lot of new friends **while** they're on holiday.*
*Safari members make a lot of new friends **during** their holiday.*

Finish the second sentence so that it means the same as the first.

1 Learn to ski before you go on a winter holiday in the mountains.
Don't go on a winter holiday in the mountains until ....

2 When we arrived at the hotel, we immediately went for a swim.
We went for a swim as ....

3 We went sightseeing after lunch.
We went sightseeing during ....

4 During my holiday in Paris, I spoke a lot of French.
I spoke a lot of French while I...

5 Don't book your holiday until you've seen my photos of Africa.
You must see my photos of Africa before ....

5 Vocabulary

You can use the words in the box when you're talking about holidays. Divide them into the six groups.

hotel countryside sunglasses shells plane taking photos swimming coach postcards train guest house car sunbathing tent suntan lotion handicrafts beach guidebook picnics

Transport	Accommodation	Scenery	Activities	Things to pack	Souvenirs
car	hotel	beach	swimming	sunglasses	postcards

Think of words which describe the kind of holiday you like most. Use a dictionary to help you. Add the words to the table.

6 Speaking

Talk about the kind of holidays you like and don't like.

3 2 Just the job

1 Speaking

Look at the people in the photo. They're all going to work.

- What do you think each person does?
- Which person earns the highest salary?
- Which person gets on well with his or her colleagues?
- Which person is responsible for a large staff?
- Which person is planning to go on strike?

2 Vocabulary

1 Many people have to study for several years before they take up a profession or job. For example, an *architect* has studied *architecture*, and a *doctor* has studied *medicine*. What have these people studied?

Profession	Subject studied
architect	*architecture*
doctor	*medicine*
lawyer	
artist	
cook	
engineer	
tourist guide	
hairdresser	
journalist	
business man/woman	
actor/actress	
chemist	
biologist	
physicist	
musician	

2 Look at these verbs. You can make nouns by changing the end of each one. Complete the table.

Verb	Noun
apply	*application*
organize	
qualify	
decide	
operate	
employ	*employment*
advertise	
govern	
manage	
retire	
insure	
succeed	

Use the pairs of words to make sentences.
Example:
If you want to apply for a job, you have to fill in an application form.

21

3 Listening

1 You will hear four women talking about their jobs. Listen and complete the information in the table.

Speaker	Clothes	Equipment	Place	Activity
1				*controlling traffic*
2			*advertising agency*	
3		*microscope*		
4				

Listen again and match the speakers with the pictures, A, B, C or D.

A

B

C

D

2 You will hear a woman talking on the radio about her job. Put a tick (✓) in the correct box for each question.

1 Where does Amanda usually work?
A ☐ in a restaurant
B ☐ in her own kitchen
C ☐ in other people's homes
D ☐ in recording studios

2 People are satisfied with Amanda's service because
A ☐ she provides large meals.
B ☐ she cooks healthy food.
C ☐ she gives people a wide choice.
D ☐ she prepares unusual dishes.

3 Amanda finds her job stressful if she
A ☐ has to cook for vegetarians.
B ☐ has to work in unsuitable places.
C ☐ doesn't know how many people to cook for.
D ☐ doesn't know when she should serve a meal.

4 What does Amanda enjoy most about her job?
A ☐ meeting famous bands
B ☐ being her own boss
C ☐ working for young people
D ☐ earning a lot of money

5 How does Amanda get to the place where she works?
A ☐ by car
B ☐ by bus
C ☐ by bike
D ☐ on foot

6 When she gets home in the evening, Amanda
A ☐ writes about cooking.
B ☐ cooks for her family.
C ☐ makes a shopping list.
D ☐ listens to music.

Get ready for PET Listening Part 2

1 Read the questions quickly before you hear the tape, so you know what to listen for.
2 You will hear the recording twice. If you miss the answer to a question, don't worry. Forget that question and think about the next one. You can find the answer when you hear the tape for a second time.
3 The answer to a question may not be in exactly the same words as the ones you hear. For example, what's the answer to question 2? What words does Amanda use to express this idea?.

4 For each question, A, B, C and D will seem possible, but only one will be right. For example, what is the answer to question 5? Amanda talks about the other kinds of transport but they are not how she gets to work. What does she say about each kind of transport?
5 Remember to check all your answers when you listen to the tape for a second time.

House and home

1 Vocabulary

1 Which rooms do you have in your house?

dining room	kitchen	bedroom	garage
living room	bathroom	hallway	balcony
garden	stairs	storeroom	basement

Do you have any other rooms in your house?

2 In which room do you usually find these things? Divide them into the four groups. Some words can be used more than once.

dishwasher	wardrobe	chest of drawers	sink
coffee table	washbasin	armchair	dressing table
television	lamp	fridge	shower
cooker	towel rail	mirror	sofa

Living room	Kitchen	Bathroom	Bedroom

2 Speaking

1 In the Speaking test, you talk about a photograph. If you don't know the English word for something, you can say what it:
- is used for
- is made of
- looks like

a) What's it used for? Read the example and complete 1–2.
Example:

What's a coffee table?
It's a small, low table which you usually find in the living room. You can put things like cups of coffee, newspapers and magazines on it.

1 What's a chest of drawers?
   It's a small piece of furniture which ....
2 What's a towel rail?
   It's..

b) What's it made of? Read the example and complete 1–2.
Example:

A wardrobe is usually made of wood.

1 A towel is usually ....
2 A frying pan is...

c) What's the difference? Read the example and complete 1–2.
Example:

dishwasher/washing machine
They are both machines which you usually find in the kitchen. A dishwasher is for washing plates, cups, etc. and a washing machine is for washing clothes.

1 cushions/pillows
2 curtains/blinds

2 Choose one of the photographs and describe the room.

A

B

Use the words in the box to help you talk about:

- the type of room it is
- what you can see in the room
- where the things are
- your opinion of the room
- who you think lives there

> there's a/some
> on top of
> next to/beside
> underneath/below
> to the right of
> to the left of
> behind
> in front of

3 Listening    **1 Listen to a boy describing his room. Which room is his?**

A ☐   B ☐   C ☐   D ☐

2 Listen to a girl describing her home. Where does she live?

A ☐   B ☐   C ☐   D ☐

3 Describe your house. Talk about:

- where it is
- what it looks like
- how many rooms it has
- your favourite room

4 Listening

Remember:
1 the pictures may be partly right and partly wrong.
2 only one picture is completely right.
3 you hear everything twice.

1 Look at the four pictures. Where is the calculator in each picture? Listen and decide which picture, A, B, C, or D, matches what you hear.

A ☐   B ☐   C ☐   D ☐

2 What time does the man's bus leave?

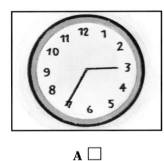 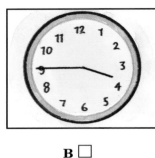 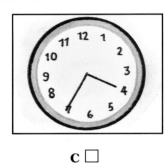 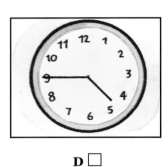

A ☐   B ☐   C ☐   D ☐

3 What does the woman decide to eat?

 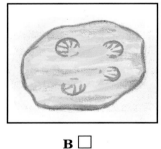  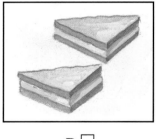

A ☐   B ☐   C ☐   D ☐

4 Which piece of equipment does the woman need?

 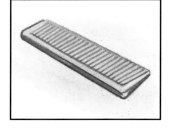  

A ☐   B ☐   C ☐   D ☐

Interesting people

1 How often does your family get together for a celebration? Do you enjoy family parties? Why? Why not?

2 Find someone in the photo who:

is bald	has long hair	is in a white dress	is smiling
is middle-aged	looks bored	is wearing a hat	is dancing

Now describe the photo. Begin like this:

'This is a picture of a family party. There are a lot of people here. Most of them are sitting down at long tables, but some people...'

3 The words in the boxes describe people. In the first box, find seven pairs of words with *opposite* meanings.

attractive	careful	careless	cheerful	confident	miserable	foolish
hard-working	lazy	shy	strong	ugly	weak	wise

4 In this box, find seven pairs of words with *similar* meanings.

amusing	anxious	blond	boring	understanding	dull	fair
funny	honest	patient	slim	thin	truthful	worried

5 Which words describe you?

Write this letter.
- You recently went to a party and made two new friends.
- Now you are writing a letter to an English friend.
- Explain who you met at the party, describe what they looked like, and say why you liked them.
- Write about 100 words.

Complete these sentences and use them in your letter.

I noticed X and Y as soon as I went in the room because ....

It's the first time I've met people who ....

X isn't good-looking but ....

Y was wearing ....

X and I liked each other immediately because ....

I got on well with Y because ....

Begin your letter like this:

Dear Sam,
I want to tell you about two people I met at a party last Saturday. ....
....

3 Reading

1 **Generally, how old are people when they first a) learn to read? b) go to university? Read the article about a boy who has done these things at a younger age than most people, and then answer the questions.**

The most difficult thing for university student Shaun Rogers is opening his classroom door. Shaun can't do this without help because he's only six years old. He's the youngest person ever to study at Rochester University in New York. Shaun began reading at two, by the age of five was regularly corresponding with university professors and will shortly complete his first book. 'I love learning,' says Shaun. 'My hero is the scientist Albert Einstein because he never combed his hair or wore socks.'

Psychologists have found it difficult to test Shaun's intelligence because it goes beyond what they usually measure. Shaun's mother first realized her son was different when he kept crying at playschool because he was bored with the children's games. She started teaching him at home after finding that local schools were not prepared for children who learnt at Shaun's speed. Now Shaun is studying geography at Rochester University and using the Internet to complete his high school studies.

However, some psychologists warn that too much study can prevent a child from developing normally. 'I don't care how brilliant the kid is, six-year-olds have to play with their friends,' says Dr Brian Wood. Mrs Rogers disagrees that her son's time is completely taken up by school work. 'He loves the violin and has many outdoor interests, such as camping, fishing and swimming, just like other boys his age.'

1 What is the writer trying to do in the text?
A advise parents about their children's education
B compare the development of normal and clever children
C encourage students to enter university at a young age
D interest people in the life of an unusual child

2 What can a reader find out from this text?
A who Shaun's friends are
B when Shaun did an intelligence test
C what Shaun's hobbies are
D how well Shaun plays the violin

3 Why did Shaun's mother decide to educate him at home?
A because she couldn't find a suitable school for him
B because his school wouldn't let him use the Internet
C because his teachers were unkind and made him cry
D because he didn't get on with the other children

4 What does Dr Wood think about Shaun?
A He isn't really any cleverer than other six-year-olds.
B He should spend more time having fun with other children.
C He will have to study harder to succeed at university.
D He can help his friends to do better at school.

5 Which of these is Mrs Rogers talking about Shaun?

A 'My son gets bored easily if he doesn't have other children to play games or go swimming with him.'

B 'My son loves his studies and fortunately there are many children of his own age in his class who share his interests.'

C 'What makes my son different from other children is that he started studying earlier and learns things much more quickly.'

D 'Like most young boys, my son often looks untidy and spends more time using the Internet than doing his homework.'

Get ready for PET Reading Part 4

1 The first question on this kind of reading text asks you about the writer's purpose in writing the text.
Has the writer of the text about Shaun succeeded in her/his purpose? In other words, has s/he interested you in Shaun's life?

2 In this kind of reading text, you have to understand people's *attitudes* and *opinions* as well as factual information. From this text, what do you understand about:

- Shaun's *attitude* to studying?
- Dr Wood's *opinion* about what six-year-old children need to do?
- Mrs Rogers' *opinion* about the amount of time her son spends studying?

3 In some of the questions in this kind of reading text, you have to look for the answer in more than one place. Look at question 5 and underline the two places in the text which give you the correct answer.

2 Match the writer's purposes with the sentences.

1 to recommend something	**A** Couples who decide to adopt a child should be prepared for the time when the child starts to ask difficult questions about the birth parents.
2 to compare two things	**B** Why do people using mobile phones in public places imagine everyone is interested in their conversations and speak in very loud voices?
3 to complain about something	**C** If, like me, you enjoy a film which keeps you sitting on the edge of your seat, then you shouldn't miss this one.
4 to explain something	**D** I felt close to my grandmother because she always met me from school and listened while I described the events of my day.
5 to warn against something	**E** Children with several brothers and sisters may feel differently from an only child when it comes to the school holidays.

4 Grammar

Finish the second sentence so that it means the same as the first.

1 That teacher is very patient with her students.
That is the teacher ....

2 Shaun is too weak to open the classroom door.
Shaun isn't...

3 In our class, only a few students have curly hair.
In our class, not ....

4 My brother prefers funny films to serious ones.
My brother likes funny films ....

5 My grandmother's favourite film star is Tom Cruise.
Tom Cruise is the film star my grandmother ....

Places of interest

1 Look at the notices, 1–10. Would you find them in a museum, a sportscentre, a hotel, a giftshop or a post office?

1
Last collection:
19.30 Mon–Fri.

2
Changing rooms this way

3
Rooms should be vacated by 12.00

4
Ask for our free gift-wrapping service

5
Parcels and heavy items should be taken to window 7 for weighing

6
Please do not touch the exhibits

7
EQUIPMENT CAN BE HIRED BY THE HOUR

8
All breakages must be paid for

9
Photocopying facilities are available to guests at Reception

10
A map of the display areas is available at the entrance

2 Look at each notice again. Is it:

a) giving you information about what facilities are available?
b) telling you what you must or mustn't do?
c) giving you simple information, for example where or when?

3 Choose one place from the box below. What type of notices would you expect to see there? Write two examples of each type, a), b) and c).

school	department store	bank	airport

Get ready for PET Listening Part 3

1 In Part 3 of the PET Listening test, you have to listen and write the missing words in the gaps on the question paper.
2 The information on the page may be presented in different ways. Make sure you know what to do. Read the information on the page carefully and think about the type of information that is missing.

3 You don't have to understand every word – just listen for the missing information.
4 You will hear the words you need to write on the tape and you don't need to change them in any way. Don't worry if you're not sure how to spell the words correctly, but make sure you write clearly.
5 Don't write too much. One or two words is usually enough.

1 Look at the notes about Orford Castle. Some information is missing.

- You will hear a recorded message about the castle.
- For each question, fill in the missing information in the numbered space.

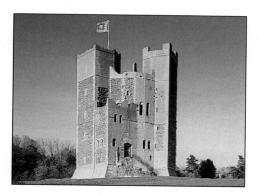

ORFORD CASTLE

Opening time:	(1) ....
Closing time:	4 pm
Price for adults:	£2.30
Price for children:	(2) ....
Telephone number:	(3) 01394 ....

In this example, the words on the left tell you what information you are listening for. Some of the information has already been completed. You only have to fill in the missing information where there is a number in brackets and a dotted line.

2 Look at the notes about Framlingham Castle. Some information is missing.

- You will hear a recorded message about the castle.
- For each question, fill in the missing information in the numbered space.

FRAMLINGHAM CASTLE

When you can go there:
Open between April and (1) ....
Open every day from 10.00 am to
(2) ....
What you can do there:
Walk around the (3) ....
Visit the (4) ....

In this example, the information is organized under headings. Again, some of the information is given and you just fill in the missing words.

3 Look at the notes about Castle Rising. Some information is missing.

- You will hear a recorded message about the castle.
- For each question, fill in the missing information in the numbered space.

CASTLE RISING

You can visit the castle any day between
(1) .... and Sunday.
There is a free (2) .... to give you
information about the castle.
In the giftshop, you can buy a
(3) .... as a souvenir of your visit.

In this example, the information about the castle is presented in the form of sentences. So, once again, some of the information is given and you just fill in the missing words.

3 Reading

Look at the statements about the trip to Arundel Castle. Read the text and decide if each statement is correct or incorrect.

1   Arundel Castle is in the same town as the Albion Hotel.
2   If you go on the trip, you may miss your evening meal at the hotel.
3   There is no charge for the journey to Arundel.
4   Arundel Castle is next to the river, in the centre of the town.
5   All of the castle buildings are less than 1,000 years old.
6   Part of the castle is in a poor condition.
7   Part of the castle is used as a private house.
8   It is necessary to book a table if you want to have lunch at the castle.
9   Afternoon tea at the castle is not very expensive.
10   To go on the trip, you have to reserve a place one day in advance.

BRITANNIA HOLIDAYS

Extra trip to Arundel Castle: Wednesday

Dear Holiday-maker,

I hope that you are enjoying your visit to the Albion Hotel. I'm writing to tell you about an extra trip we are arranging for Wednesday afternoon. We'll be going to Arundel Castle, which is a tourist attraction about 40 miles from here. A coach will be leaving at 11 am and returning in time for your evening meal at 7 pm. The kitchen has been informed so if we're late for any reason, they'll wait for us. Please remember this is not part of your package so, although the coach is free, there is an entrance fee of £7.00 if you want to visit the castle.

The town of Arundel is very pretty, with pleasant walks down by the river and some interesting old shops. The castle stands on a hill outside the town and can be seen from miles around. There has been a castle on this site for almost 1,000 years, but the present building is not that old, so it's certainly not an old ruin. The castle buildings are used as a home by the present owners, but quite a large part is open to the public.

Among the things to see at the castle are some lovely rooms. The library has a wonderful ceiling and there is a beautiful bedroom, once used by members of the royal family. There is furniture dating from the 16th century and a fine collection of old clocks, which shouldn't be missed. The picture gallery is also very interesting and has paintings by famous artists such as Canaletto and Gainsborough.

We will arrive in Arundel at lunchtime and the castle has its own restaurant, which serves excellent home-made lunches. If a group of you would like to pre-book, we can arrange a discount for you. If not, you can decide when you arrive and there are always plenty of free tables. For those of you who prefer a lighter meal, traditional English afternoon tea is served in the restaurant from 3.00 pm at a very reasonable price.

So, if you would like to join us on our trip to Arundel, please ask at Reception by Tuesday lunchtime at the latest, and your name will be added to the list.
Have a nice day.

Clara Tongue
Tour Company Representative

4 Speaking

1   **What are the main tourist attractions in your area**
• for young people?
• for older people?
• for foreign visitors?

2   **Talk about a historic building in your country and say what visitors can see and do there.**

Getting there

1 Vocabulary

1 Look at the words in the box. Divide them into four groups. Some of the words can be used more than once.

driver	pilot	attendant	land	catch	miss
get on	take off	check in	ticket	fare	station
take	platform	boarding pass	meter	timetable	gate

Taxi	Train	Bus/Coach	Plane

2 Complete the gaps in these sentences with words from the table.

1 If we don't hurry up, we'll .... the bus. It leaves the bus .... at ten o'clock.
2 It's cheaper for four people to .... a taxi rather than go on the underground, because the taxi .... comes to less than the price of four ....
3 After you .... your luggage, they give you a .... which you take along to the .... , where someone checks it before you .... the plane.
4 The train to Edinburgh leaves from .... number eight and you have to buy your .... in the office before you ....
5 In the .... , it said that the bus left at 10.00, and so we got there at 09.45 so that we would be sure to .... it.

2 Speaking

Look at the photograph and describe it. Make sure you answer these questions:

* Where was it taken? Who are the people? What is each of them doing? Why?
* What things can you see in the photograph?
* What are the people going to do next? Why?

What are the good and bad things about travelling by plane?

3 Reading

1 Look at these notices. On which type of transport would you expect to see each one?

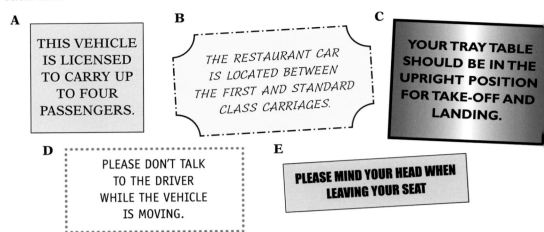

A

THIS VEHICLE
IS LICENSED
TO CARRY UP
TO FOUR
PASSENGERS.

B

THE RESTAURANT CAR
IS LOCATED BETWEEN
THE FIRST AND STANDARD
CLASS CARRIAGES.

C

YOUR TRAY TABLE
SHOULD BE IN THE
UPRIGHT POSITION
FOR TAKE-OFF AND
LANDING.

D

PLEASE DON'T TALK
TO THE DRIVER
WHILE THE VEHICLE
IS MOVING.

E

PLEASE MIND YOUR HEAD WHEN
LEAVING YOUR SEAT

Get ready for PET Reading Part 1

1 In Part 1 of the PET Reading test, there are five multiple-choice (**A**, **B**, **C**, or **D**) questions.

2 Remember that notices may be:
- telling you what to do or what not to do.
- telling you what is available.
- giving you information about things.

3 This is how to choose the correct explanation.
- First, look at the sign and imagine how you would explain it to a friend.
- Then look at the four explanations and choose the one which is closest to what you would say.
- Finally, check the other explanations and find words or phrases in the notice that tell you that these explanations are not correct.

2 Look at this notice. Choose the correct explanation, A, B, C or D.

Available 1st July.
One-bedroom furnished flat.
Reasonable rent.
Convenient for shops
and buses.

A I'm looking for somewhere to live.
B I'm looking for furniture for a flat.
C I'm looking for someone to live in a flat.
D I'm looking for someone who wants to buy a flat.

The answer to this question is **C**.
Which words tell you that this is the answer?
Which words tell you that **A** is not the answer?
Which words tell you that **B** is not the answer?
Which words tell you that **D** is not the answer?

3 Look at these notices and decide which is the correct explanation, A, B, C or D. Think about why your answer is correct and why the other explanations are not correct.

1

PLEASE SPEAK
QUIETLY IN THE
LIBRARY AREA.
PEOPLE ARE
STUDYING NEARBY.

A You are not allowed to talk here.
B You can only stay here if you are studying.
C You should try not to disturb people.
D You may only speak in certain parts of the library.

2

GARDEN PARTY
1st June 11.30–16.00
LAST FEW TICKETS
£5.00

A Have you lost your ticket?
B Does anybody else want to come?
C Have you paid for your ticket?
D Can anyone sell me a ticket?

3

Hot and cold snacks served all day.

A You can help yourself if you are hungry.
B Sit down and a waiter will come to serve you.
C You can buy drinks here, but not food.
D You can get a light meal here.

4

THIS CAR PARK IS RESERVED FOR MEMBERS OF STAFF.

A You can only park here if you work here.
B You can only park here at certain times.
C You can only park here for short periods.
D You can only park here if you book in advance.

5

ALL VISITORS SHOULD REPORT TO THE OFFICE ON ARRIVAL.

A Please go to the office before you leave.
B Please call the office to make an appointment.
C Please go to the office when you first come here.
D Please call the office if you cannot visit us.

---

4 Writing

You have been asked to complete a questionnaire about travelling in your country. Look at the questionnaire and answer each question.

TRAVEL QUESTIONNAIRE

1 Surname: ....

2 Forenames: ....

3 Home address: ....

4 Are you are a car driver? ....

5 How do you usually travel to work/school/college?.....................................

6 How many hours a week do you spend travelling? ....

7 What is good about the way you travel?...

8 What is not so good about the way you travel?...

9 What alternatives are available to you? ....

10 Signature: ....

Thank you for taking time to fill in this questionnaire.

What a bargain!

What's the difference between these pairs of words?
Example:
A jacket is shorter than a coat.
Check your answers in a dictionary.

coat/jacket	shirt/skirt
boot/shoe	socks/tights
tie/belt	wool/cotton
collar/sleeve	spots/stripes
pocket/bag	zip/buttons

Read these notices. Match them with the correct explanation, A, B, C, or D. There is one extra explanation.

1

> **Changing rooms next to lift.**
> **Customers may take in no more than 4 pieces of clothing.**

2

> Sorry!
> Lift to women's fashions out of order –
> Use escalator in TV department

3

> Today only!
> Prices on all electrical goods greatly reduced

A Because the lift isn't working, you'll have to go upstairs another way.
B You may not change any women's clothes you buy in today's sale.
C If you buy a television today, it will be much cheaper than usual.
D There's a limit to the number of clothes you may try on at one time.

Read the sentences about money and find the missing words in the word square. They are written from top to bottom, left to right, right to left and diagonally.

1 I don't _ _ _ _ a lot of money in my job, but I _ _ _ _ some every week for my holiday.
2 If you don't have cash, you can write a _ _ _ _ _ _ or pay by _ _ _ _ _ _ card.
3 If you don't put that _ _ _ _ in your wallet, and the _ _ _ _ in your pocket, you'll lose them before you can spend them!

C	S	L	S	A	V	E
H	C	H	E	Q	U	E
A	O	R	O	N	X	A
R	I	W	E	P	D	R
G	N	X	E	D	I	N
E	T	O	N	P	I	T
R	E	C	E	I	P	T

4 I got a _ _ _ _ _ _ _ when I bought these books for you, so you can see how much money you _ _ _ me.
5 Some people will borrow money from you, but they'll never _ _ _ _ it to you!
6 People like to _ _ _ _ in big department stores because everything they want is under one roof.
7 How much do you _ _ _ _ _ _ to repair shoes?
8 The service was very good here, so I'm going to leave the waitress a large _ _ _ .

4 Writing

1 **In PET Writing Part 3, you are asked to write a letter to an English-speaking friend. Look at this example writing task.**

- On your birthday recently, you received a present from an English-speaking friend.
- Now you are writing a letter to this friend.
- Thank your friend for the present, invite your friend to visit a new shopping centre with you, and describe the shopping centre.
- Write about 100 words.

2 **This is the letter one student wrote. Write the missing words.**

Dear Chris,

Thank you very [1] .... for the birthday present [2] .... sent me. It [3] .... kind of you to remember [4] .... birthday. The sweater [5] .... me perfectly and I love the colour. I'm going [6] .... use the money my grandmother gave me to buy some new trousers to go [7] .... it.

Have you [8] .... to the new shopping centre yet? Why don't [9] .... go together this Saturday? I could come [10] .... your house at about 3 o'clock and then we could [11] .... the bus from the end [12] .... your street.

I know you'll like [13] .... shopping centre. It has a [14] .... of really good clothes shops, great music stores, and [15] .... enormous bookstore. There's a café [16] .... we can have ice cream, and, [17] .... we've got any money left, we [18] .... see a film at the cinema there.

I [19] .... you can come. Phone me or [20] .... me an e-mail.

Love,
Andrea

- How does Andrea thank Chris? What does Andrea say about the sweater?
- How does Andrea invite Chris?
- Look at these sentences. Find three invitations, one acceptance, and one refusal.
  Please come to the shopping centre with me.
  I'd really like you to come to the shopping centre with me.
  I'd love to go to the shopping centre with you.
  Would you like to come to the shopping centre with me?
  I'm afraid I can't go to the shopping centre with you.
- You make arrangements when you give an invitation. What arrangements does Andrea suggest?
- At the end of a letter, you write one or two 'goodbye' sentences.
  How does Andrea show the letter includes an invitation?
  What other 'goodbye' sentence does Andrea write?
- Look at these sentences. Find four 'goodbye' sentences and one 'hello' sentence.
  Please write soon.
  I'm sorry I haven't written for a long time.
  Thank you again for the lovely present.
  Give my love/best wishes to your family.
  See you soon.
- At the end of a letter, you always sign your name. What does Andrea write before the signature? Look at these phrases. Find two from an informal letter and one from a formal one.
  Yours sincerely,
  Best wishes,
  Yours,

Get ready for PET Writing Part 3

1 Read the instructions carefully and imagine yourself in the situation.
2 In your letter, you are told to do three things. For example, in the letter to Chris, you have to *thank*, *invite* and *describe*. Make sure you follow the instructions for all three of them.
3 Your letter will look good if you write it in separate paragraphs, as Andrea has done. Start each paragraph on a new line.
4 Remember to write a 'goodbye' sentence and to sign your name.
5 Try not to write fewer than 100 words, but don't write many more than 100.
6 When you've written your letter, check it carefully. Make sure you've followed all the instructions. Correct any grammar and spelling mistakes.

3 Write this letter.

- You spent last Saturday with an English-speaking friend and this friend has just sent you some photos of the day.
- Now you are writing a letter to this friend.
- Thank your friend for the photos, invite your friend to visit a local tourist attraction with you next weekend, and describe what you can see and do there.
- Write about 100 words.

Dear Lesley,
I've just received the photos you took last Saturday. ....
....

5 Listening 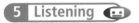   **Do you like shopping in street markets? Why? Why not?**
- Look at the advertisement for some street markets in London.
- Some information is missing.
- Listen to the man talking on the radio about the markets, and fill in the missing words.

East London Markets

Columbia Road
Over 50 stalls selling (1) .... at bargain prices.

Brick Lane
A market speciality is (2) ....

Petticoat Lane
Sells everything from clothes to toys. Busiest day is (3) ....

Whitechapel
It's opposite (4) .... Get your Asian vegetables and spices here.

Come and be part of the fun!

City life

1 ⟨ Vocabulary ⟩

1 Look at these photographs. Choose one of the photographs and make a list of all the things you can see. Use the ideas to help you.

A    B

people

colours

objects

clothes

parts of the vehicle

buildings

2 Answer these questions about your photograph.

1 What type of vehicle is it?
2 What type of street is it?
3 What are the people in the photo doing?
4 Why are they doing it?
5 How do you think they feel about it?

3 Now look at the other photograph and answer these questions.

1 What's the same or similar?
2 What's different?

2 ⟨ Speaking ⟩

1 Which is better, living in a city or living in the country? Why?

2 Look at the adjectives in the box. Which would you use to describe
a) living in the city? b) living in the country?

calm	crowded	peaceful	clean	noisy
dirty	boring	relaxing	stressful	convenient
expensive	exciting	safe	lonely	interesting
fun	dangerous	polluted	inconvenient	

3 Make lists of the advantages of living in a) the city and b) the country. Use the words in the box to help you.

shopping	night-life	fresh air	way of life	education
employment	transport	health		entertainment

4 **Talk to another student. Decide who is Student A and who is Student B. Use your lists to have a discussion about life in the two places. Use some of the expressions below.**

Student A
Try to convince your partner that the city is the best place to live.

Student B
Try to convince your partner that the country is the best place to live.

One big (dis)advantage of the city/country is that...

But we have to remember that it is easier to ...... in the city/country.

Don't forget that the city/country is much more ...... than the country/city.

Another thing is that the city/country is better for...

I'm afraid I don't agree with you because...

Yes, you're right, but I still think...

Get ready for PET Speaking Part 3

1 In Part 3 of the PET Speaking test, you have to talk about a photograph which shows an everyday situation.
2 You have to tell the examiner what you can see in the picture. You talk for less than a minute.

3 Remember:
- start immediately, and keep talking – don't stop and think.
- talk to the examiner, not your partner.
- talk about everything you can see.
- say if you like the photograph or not.
- if you don't know a word, don't stop – talk about something else.
- listen when your partner is talking.

5 **When you talk about the photograph, use these ideas to help you.**

1 Talk about the *place* in the photograph.
- Is it indoors or outdoors?
- Is it in a house or another building?
- What type of place is it?

2 Talk about the *people* in the photograph.
- How many people are there?
- What do they look like?
- What are they wearing?
- How do they feel?

3 Talk about *what's happening* in the photograph.
- What are the people doing?
- Why are they doing it?

6 Look at the photograph of some people in the countryside. Talk about it using the ideas in 5.

7 Look at the photograph of people in a city and talk about it. Remember:

- don't talk for more than one minute
- talk about everything you can see in the picture
- don't worry about words you don't know

8 Talk about a city you know. Say what you like about it and what you don't like about it.

7 Food and drink

1 Vocabulary

1 Look at the foods in the box. Divide them into the four groups.

carrots	beans	lamb	peas	onions	garlic
mushrooms	bananas	sausages	grapes	tomatoes	oranges
duck	pasta	beef	rice	chicken	leeks
olives	mayonnaise	tuna	butter	cheese	spinach
pepper	salt	steak	pizza	plums	burgers

Meat and fish	Vegetables	Fruit	Other

2 Add your favourite foods to the lists.

2 Speaking

1 Choose one of the photographs of people eating and talk about it. Remember to talk about everything you can see, including:
- each person – what they are doing, wearing and feeling
- the food and drink
- other things in the foreground
- things in the background

A

B

2 What is your favourite food? Talk about:

- breakfast
- dinner
- a snack
- a special meal
- a special treat

What do you drink with these foods?

Get ready for PET Speaking Part 4

1 In Part 4 of the PET Speaking test, you have a conversation with your partner. You only have a few minutes for the task.
2 The examiner tells you what to talk about, but does not ask you any questions.
3 The topic of Part 4 is the same as the one in the pictures in Part 3.

4 Remember:
- talk to your partner, not to the examiner
- ask your partner questions
- listen and respond to what your partner says
- don't talk for too long, and give your partner a chance to speak.

3 Look at the photographs again and listen to the examiner's instructions for the Part 4 task. What is the topic of the conversation? Make a list of the things you can talk about and the questions you can ask your partner. Think about how to begin the conversation.

Have the conversation with another student.

4 Listen to two students beginning the task. As you listen, think about:

- how they begin
- how long each person speaks for
- how they show interest in what each other says

5 Work with another student and do this Part 4 task. Don't talk for too long without involving your partner! Remember to ask questions and show interest. Use some of these phrases.

That's interesting because...

I like ...... , don't you?

I agree with you about that.

Really?

So do I!

Me too, and another thing is...

What about you?

Talk together about good restaurants you have been to and what you like to eat there.

3 Vocabulary

1 Look at the picture. Can you complete the gaps in this list of ingredients?

some different-sized ....   a hard-boiled ....
a small tin of ....   some black ....
two spoonfuls of ....   two spoonfuls of ....

**What equipment do you think
you need to make this recipe?**

 Now listen and check your ideas.

2 How do you think you make this
recipe? Use these verbs and the
ingredients above to talk about it.

cut	mix	stir
pour	take out	

*First you
have to...*   *Then you...*   *Finally you...*

Now listen and check your ideas. Complete the table as you listen.

	Equipment	Verb	Ingredients
1			
2			
3			
4			
5			
6			
7			

4 Grammar

Finish the second sentence so that it means the same as the first.
1 In our house, the salad is usually prepared by my brother.
  In our house, my brother usually ....
2 At breakfast, all the orange juice was drunk.
  At breakfast, someone ....
3 My mother told me not to burn the rice.
  My mother said, 'Don't ....
4 In the restaurant, Robbie asked for a burger with chips.
  In the restaurant, Robbie said, 'Can ....
5 Martine suggested we ordered a pizza.
  Martine said, 'Let's ....

1 Speaking

Talk about how important each of these things is for you at home:
1 a room or space which is your own
2 a quiet place where you can relax or study
3 a place where you can make as much noise as you like
4 a place where you can invite your friends in comfort
5 your own special seat at the dining table
6 somewhere outside, for example a balcony or garden

2 Reading

1 **Read this text about teenagers. Choose the correct word, A, B, C or D, for each space.**

PERSONAL SPACE

More and more people live in large cities these days and this means that it is becoming more and more difficult to find space and time for ourselves. But for many people, personal privacy is very important. In many homes, a few minutes in the bathroom is all the privacy that is **(1)** ....

Teenagers especially need their own personal space at home where they can feel relaxed and private. But, of course, not all teenagers are **(2)** .... enough to have a room of their own. Where space is short, they often have to **(3)** .... a bedroom with a brother or sister. In that case, it's a good **(4)** .... for them to have a special area or corner of the room to **(5)** .... their own. It's especially important for young people to have somewhere to **(6)** .... their personal things. This may or may not be a tidy place and it is not a good idea for parents to try and tell teenagers how to **(7)** .... their space as this is **(8)** .... to lead to arguments. Parents can, however, **(9)** .... sure that there are enough storage spaces such as shelves, cupboards and boxes. This will **(10)** .... the teenager to keep their space tidy if they want to.

1	**A** confident	**B** available	**C** general	**D** average
2	**A** dizzy	**B** early	**C** lucky	**D** happy
3	**A** separate	**B** share	**C** divide	**D** join
4	**A** sense	**B** opinion	**C** idea	**D** thought
5	**A** mind	**B** call	**C** say	**D** tell
6	**A** belong	**B** save	**C** support	**D** keep
7	**A** organize	**B** repair	**C** operate	**D** review
8	**A** really	**B** quickly	**C** actually	**D** likely
9	**A** find	**B** make	**C** get	**D** put
10	**A** afford	**B** let	**C** allow	**D** set

2 Read the complete text again and answer these questions.

1 What is the writer trying to do in this text?
A complain about something
B blame someone for something
C give advice about something
D warn people about something

2 What does the writer believe?
A Teenagers can be selfish.
B Everybody needs some privacy.
C Parents can be unreasonable.
D Sharing is more important than privacy.

3 What does the writer think about tidiness?
A It is important for teenagers to be tidy.
B It is possible even when space is limited.
C It's a waste of time trying to be tidy.
D Parents should make their children be tidy.

3 Listening

Get ready for PET Listening Part 4

1 Part 4 of the PET Listening test is always a conversation between two people. They will be giving their opinions about something, and agreeing or disagreeing with each other.

2 Remember to read the instructions carefully to find out:
• who is talking
• where they are
• what they are talking about.
This will help you to imagine the situation and understand what they say.

3 Remember to read the statements on the question paper carefully to:
• make sure you know whose opinion the statement is about
• check if the statement matches the text or not.

4 You may not understand all the words in the text. Don't worry, you only have to answer six questions with YES or NO. If you're not sure, guess. You have a 50 per cent chance of being right!

1 Read the instructions for this Part 4 task.

• Look at the six statements for this part.
• You will hear a conversation between a man, Bob, and a woman, Mary. They are talking about their teenage children.
• Decide if you think each statement is correct or incorrect.
• If you think it is correct, put a tick (✓) in the box under **A** for **YES**. If you think it is incorrect, put a tick (✓) in the box under **B** for **NO**.

2 Now listen and complete the task.

	A YES	B No
1 Mary's house is too small for Matthew to have his own room.	☐	☐
2 Matthew is a lot younger than his brother.	☐	☐
3 Bob wanted to spend more time alone as a teenager.	☐	☐
4 Matthew would like to have his own computer.	☐	☐
5 Mary feels that Matthew's brother has more need of a computer.	☐	☐
6 Matthew would like to watch the television more.	☐	☐

4 **Speaking**

What do you think?

1 How do you organize your personal space?
2 Do people respect your personal space?
3 Do you respect other people's space?
4 Do you think that tidiness is important?

5 **Listening**

Now do this task.

• Look at the six statements.
• Alice and Harry are talking about their personal space.
• As you listen, decide if each statement is correct or incorrect.
• If you think it is correct, put a tick (✓) in the box under **A** for **YES**. If you think it is incorrect, put a tick (✓) in the box under **B** for **NO**.

	A YES	B No
1 Alice regrets arguing with her mother.	☐	☐
2 Alice thinks her mother should put clothes away for her.	☐	☐
3 Alice tidies her room when she's expecting visitors.	☐	☐
4 Alice's wardrobe is too small for all her clothes.	☐	☐
5 Harry sometimes lets his brother wear his clothes.	☐	☐
6 Harry and his brother have to share a bedroom.	☐	☐

6 **Speaking**

Look at the two photographs. Talk about what you can see in each room.

A

B

Close to nature

**Use the words in the box to complete this text about the environment.
Write one word in each space.**

breathe	destroying	dusty	fuels	inhabitants	minerals
poverty	prevent	rescue	rubbish	spoil	urgent

STOP DAMAGING THE EARTH!

We have spent the last one hundred years **(1)** .... our environment. In cities, factories and cars pollute the air we **(2)** .... , and everything we touch is **(3)** .... and dirty. We **(4)** .... the countryside by throwing away our **(5)** .... there, and ruin areas of natural beauty by digging up **(6)** .... , such as iron and gold, and **(7)** .... , such as coal and oil. While some people get rich, others suffer from **(8)** .... , hunger and disease. We must **(9)** .... this situation from getting worse. Finding a way to **(10)** .... our planet is an extremely **(11)** .... problem for all the **(12)** .... of the world.

---

1 Last Saturday three people went out for the day. They each took a photograph.

A   B   C

Listen to the three people talking about the weather on their day out and decide which photo each person took.

Speaker 1 ....   Speaker 2 ....   Speaker 3 ....

2 Listen to the three speakers again and write down all the weather words they use.

Good weather	Bad weather	Other weather words
fine	*storms*	*forecast*

Talk about:
- weather that makes you feel cheerful/depressed
- clothes you wear in different kinds of weather
- activities you do in different kinds of weather
- the weather and holidays, celebrations and sports events

4 Reading

Read this text about giraffes. Choose the correct word, A, B, C or D, for each space.

THE GIRAFFE

Giraffes are the tallest of all animals. When it is born, a baby giraffe **(1)** .... about 1.7 metres and it grows to 5.3 metres in height. The giraffe has a strong and **(2)** .... long tongue (40 cm) which it uses to **(3)** .... leaves off trees. A giraffe **(4)** .... most of the water it needs from leaves and so it can go for more than a month **(5)** .... drinking. When it has a drink, it has to stand with its front legs wide apart in order to **(6)** .... the water. If it needs to **(7)** .... itself, it does so by kicking, but it has **(8)** .... enemies. A lion may jump on a giraffe if one passes under the tree **(9)** .... the lion is sitting, but giraffes have such good eyesight they usually **(10)** .... the lion in time.

1	**A** measures	**B** weighs	**C** looks	**D** appears
2	**A** greatly	**B** much	**C** extremely	**D** too
3	**A** put	**B** carry	**C** bring	**D** tear
4	**A** holds	**B** gets	**C** picks	**D** keeps
5	**A** except	**B** until	**C** through	**D** without
6	**A** reach	**B** arrive	**C** come	**D** move
7	**A** fight	**B** defend	**C** strike	**D** attack
8	**A** little	**B** any	**C** few	**D** other
9	**A** which	**B** where	**C** how	**D** that
10	**A** notice	**B** realize	**C** mind	**D** watch

Get ready for PET Reading Part 5

1 First read through the whole text to get a good idea of the general meaning.

2 Sometimes your knowledge of *vocabulary* is tested, for example in 4. Only one of these verbs (*holds*, *gets*, *picks*, *keeps*) makes sense in this sentence. Try each one in the space before you decide which is the correct word.

3 Sometimes your knowledge of *grammar* is tested, for example in 8. Only one of these words (*little, any, few, other*) is correct here. Which one? Why are the other words incorrect?

4 Sometimes your knowledge of *vocabulary and grammar* is tested, for example in 6. The four words (*reach, arrive, come, move*) have similar meanings but only one is correct here. Which one? If you put *arrive, come* or *move* in the space, what other words would you need to make the sentence correct?

5 Listening 😀 **You will hear someone talking on the radio about some animals and the extraordinary things that happened to them. Put a tick [✔] against the correct answer for each question.**

1 How far did Daisy, the cow, fly on her first flight?
A across the road
B across a field
C 2 km
D 5 km

2 What kind of transport does Speedy, the cat, use?
A motorbike
B car
C bus
D bicycle

3 Who finally caught Fluffy, the cat, in the plane?
A the pilot
B a flight attendant
C a passenger
D her owner

4 When does Tom worry about his pigeon, Pete?
A when he's going fast
B when cars are overtaking
C when he's on long journeys
D when he's turning right

5 What did Rambo, the gorilla, do when the boy cried?
A He held his hand.
B He touched his face.
C He put his arm round him.
D He made noises.

6 What had happened to the boy before Prince, the dog, found him?
A He was buried by snow.
B He had fallen down a mountain.
C He couldn't get out of a river.
D He had fallen out of a tree.

6 Speaking

Discuss these questions.
1 Someone wants to give you an animal as a pet. Which one will you choose? Why?

goldfish	kitten	duck	rabbit	mouse	monkey

2 Which of these animals do you think helps humans most? Why?

bee	chicken	cow	elephant	horse	dog

3 Which of these animals would you be most afraid to meet? Why?

spider	snake	shark	bat	tiger	bear

The wide world

1 **Reading**

1 Would you like to tour a foreign country on a bicycle? Which countries do you think it would be good to visit in this way? Would tourists enjoy travelling through your country by bike?

2 Read the statements about cycling in Sri Lanka. Then read the text and decide if each statement is correct or incorrect.

1 More people in Sri Lanka ride a mountain bike than any other kind of bike.
2 The writer says that you can go a satisfactory distance each day on a bike.
3 The writer says a bicycle is a restful way of travelling through Sri Lanka.
4 The canals provide water for rice growing in spaces in the jungle.
5 The writer admired the colours of the countryside.

On two wheels in a green land

It is often said that the best way to see a country is to use the method of transport which is traditional in that particular place. So people should see Argentina on horseback, Nepal on foot and the US by car. If this is true, then a bicycle is the perfect way to visit Sri Lanka. Although the 18-speed mountain bike I used is not an everyday sight, more traditional models are popular all over the country.

Sharing the same kind of transport as local people changes the way you see the place. You are travelling at a speed that somehow fits the scenery – not so slow that you only see a small area each day, and not so fast that the details of the countryside are missed. Better still, you can stop whenever you want to listen to the birds or a waterfall, talk to people, smell their cooking or take a photo. However, this doesn't mean cycling in Sri Lanka is relaxing. If you want to see the whole country, you have to leave the towns and villages and cycle through jungle, where the temperature is 37 degrees, cross streams, climb hills and go over paths which are made of mud, rock or sand.

The most pleasant paths in the jungle follow the irrigation canals. These carry water into the bright green rice fields which appear at regular intervals among the trees. During the afternoon, groups of children, farm workers and water buffalo all come to swim in the canals. Then, when you climb from the jungle up into the hilly area in the centre of the country, you see every hillside is covered with neat rows of tea bushes in another brilliant shade of green. In fact, the whole country is covered in more different and beautiful shades of green than I ever thought possible.

Now I'm wondering where to ride my bike next – perhaps alongside the canals of The Netherlands, or through the city streets of China...

2 Vocabulary

Look at these groups of words. Which one is different?
Example:
sea   ocean   bush   lake
***bush** is different because it's not water.*

1 mountain   desert   cliff   hill
2 waterfall   country   continent   district
3 forest   wood   jungle   island
4 stream   canal   cave   river
5 bay   mud   sand   soil
6 path   road   track   wave
7 valley   coast   shore   beach
8 border   flood   frontier   edge

3 Speaking

Do you like adventure films? What difficulties and dangers do the heroes meet?
Who do you want to win in this kind of film – the heroes or the villains?
Imagine this situation.

• A famous director of adventure films wants your advice about the location of his
  next film. Here are some places where the action in the film may happen.

• Talk about the adventures the hero and heroine may have in each place
  and say which you think will be the most exciting.
• Which actors would you like to star in this film? Do you think it would be a
  popular film?

4 Grammar

1 Finish the second sentence so that it means the same as the first.

1 Britain is an island, so everywhere is near to the sea.
Britain is an island, so nowhere is ....

2 Never walk across the desert without taking water with you.
Take water with you if ....

3 Look at a map of the Indian Ocean if you want to find Sri Lanka.
You won't find Sri Lanka unless ....

4 I became a geography teacher five years ago.
I have taught ....

5 The geography teacher asked the students if they wanted to watch a video.
The geography teacher said to the students, 'Would ....

2 Now rewrite these sentences about a family going to live in a different country. Finish the second sentence so that it means the same as the first.

1 Yesterday, our passport photos were taken by a photographer.
Yesterday, a photographer ....

2 My suitcases are heavier than my brother's.
My brother's suitcases aren't ....

3 At first, we'll have great difficulty understanding the language.
At first, understanding the language will be very...

4 We have to find a flat before we can look for a school.
We can't look for a school until we ....

5 My brother and I have both promised to send e-mails to our friends.
I've promised to send e-mails to my friends and so...

Get ready for PET Writing Part 1

1 This part is a test of your grammar. Everything you write must be correct, but don't worry because you only have to write a few words.

2 The second sentence *must* have the same meaning as the first sentence.

3 There are several different kinds of changes that you have to make, but they aren't difficult. For example, sometimes you have to:

- find words with the opposite meaning. (See 1.1 above.)
- change the order of the words. (See 1.2 above.)
- change the tense of the verb. (See 1.4 above.)
- change reported speech to direct speech. (See 1.5 above.)
- make a passive sentence into an active one. (See 2.1 above.)
- change the way you compare two things. (See 2.2 above.)

4 Remember to copy any words from the first sentence very carefully! For example in 1.2 above, did you copy *across the desert* correctly?

9 1 Free time

1 Vocabulary

1 **Rearrange these letters to make the names of sports.**
Example:
TALLBOFO = football

1 FRIWGUSNNID
2 BLATTNIESEN
3 FLOG
4 STYGNIMCAS

5 DOJU
6 COKYEH
7 SEALLABB

2 **Which of these sports do you like playing? What equipment do you need?**
Which of these sports do you like watching? What skills must the players have?

2 Reading

What do you like to do in your school holidays?
- These people are all looking for a school holiday activity.
- Read the descriptions of eight school holiday activities.
- Decide which activity (letters **A–H**) would be most suitable for each person (numbers **1–5**).

1 Gwen is 18 and wants to take her younger brothers and sisters, aged between eight and 15, somewhere where they can get close to animals. She's just failed her driving test.

2 Matthew would like to take his daughter somewhere special on her sixth birthday, but he's only free in the afternoon. She loves hearing stories about animals but is frightened of real ones.

3 Lindsey has 11-year-old twin boys who hate sitting still. She wants to take them somewhere they can enjoy themselves safely all day while she goes to work.

4 Lewis is 15 and wants to do something exciting for the day with some friends from the school swimming team. They're keen to do something connected with either music or sport.

5 Jenny's going to look after her grandchildren, aged ten and seven, for the day. She can't afford to spend any money, but she'd like them to have some entertainment before she takes them home for lunch.

Holiday Fun
for Young People

A Pineapple Theatre Every day at 3 o'clock, young children (4–7 years) can watch 'Stardog'. The fun dog from space invents things to help earth people. At 5 o'clock, a group of 10–16-year-olds presents 'Football Fever', a play about young sports stars. All tickets £3.

B Queen's Arts Centre A day-long course for children (9–13 years) introduces the art of telling stories through music and poetry. Use your own history to make a musical piece. Younger children (4–8 years) may use rubbish to make musical instruments and then play them. No charge for entrance.

C Museum Gardens Circus skills workshop for children (7–11 years). Try juggling, rope walking and putting on clown make-up. Or watch Tiptop Theatre tell the story of a Native American boy and his horse. Both programmes 10–12 am. Entrance free.

D Sunshine Safari We have three floors of slides, swings, rope bridges and other adventure activities. Young adventurers can join a tiger hunt or swim with crocodiles. It all seems very real! Leave your children (3–14 years) in the care of our trained staff. £35 per day, lunch extra.

E Balloon flight See the countryside without having to drive! Our gas-filled balloon is tied to the ground and doesn't actually travel, but the views are fantastic. Price: £12 adult, £7.50 child. No under 5s, no children under 16 without an adult.

F Sea Life Centre Discover facts about life under the sea and watch many varieties of fish. The three-hour tour includes handling starfish, feeding sharks and swimming with dolphins. Adults £4.95, children £3.50.

G Making waves This adventurous programme for 12–18-year-olds gives you a chance to try your skills in a sailing boat, a canoe and a motor boat for just £12 a day. Full instruction is given. You must be a good swimmer and agree to follow all safety rules.

H Paradise Animal Park Drive your car through the park and get close to some of the world's most beautiful and dangerous animals. Younger visitors can have fun in the play area, while there is excitement for older children in the adventure playground with its 10-metre free-fall slide. Family ticket £25.

Get ready for PET Reading paper

1. You have 1 hour and 30 minutes for the Reading and Writing paper. Plan your time carefully.
2. There are five reading parts to the paper. Each part has a different kind of reading text with its own questions.
3. You can get 35 marks for the Reading paper, one mark for each question.
4. In the exam you get a question paper and an answer sheet (see p.92-3). You can make notes on the question paper but you must mark all your answers on the answer sheet.
5. You must use pencil on the answer sheet. Take a pencil, pencil sharpener and rubber to the exam.
6. Read the texts carefully but don't worry if there are words you don't understand. You probably don't need to know them to answer the questions.
7. Mark one letter for each question. To make a change, rub it out carefully and mark the new answer clearly.
8. If there is a question you can't answer, leave it and go back to it later.
9. Near the end of the test time, check your answers and make sure you have marked an answer for everything. If you don't know something, guess – you may be right!
10. There is more information about this paper in the **Get ready** boxes in this book. Make sure you read them again before the exam.

3 Vocabulary

1 These people are all planning to do their favourite free-time activity. What does each person need? Choose the words from the box.

I'm going to make a skirt to wear to the party tomorrow.

I'm going to decorate my bedroom and put up some shelves.

I'm going to answer this letter from my penfriend.

I'm going to do some work in the garden.

I'm going to have a game of tennis.

 1

 2

 3

 4

 5

balls	brush	dictionary	envelope	flower pot net
hammer	material	nails	needle	notepaper
racket	paint	scissors	pins	watering can
seeds	spade	sports bag	stamp	refreshing drink

2 What's your favourite free-time activity? What do you need to do it?

4 Speaking

A friend of yours has just moved to a different town and wants to take up a hobby that will help him/her make new friends. Here are some pictures of some hobbies he/she could do.

- Talk about how interesting the different hobbies are, and decide which will be best for making friends.

9 ② Get well soon!

1 Writing

1 Do you think you have a healthy lifestyle? What makes your lifestyle healthy or unhealthy?

2 Answer the questions on the healthy lifestyle survey.

> ## Healthy Lifestyle Survey
> Modern Living Magazine, PO Box 101, Leeds, UK
>
> **Do people today lead healthy lives? Please answer our questions.**
>
> Full name: **(1)** ....
> Age: **(2)** ....
> Sex: **(3)** ....
> Height (in metres): **(4)** ....
> Weight (in kilos): **(5)** ....
> How many hours do you sleep each night? **(6)** ....
> What kind of exercise do you do regularly? **(7)** ....
> What did you have for breakfast today? **(8)** ....
> What unhealthy habit do you have which you should give up?
> **(9)** ....
> When you feel under stress, how do you relax?
> **(10)** ....

Compare your answers with some other students. Who do you think has the healthiest lifestyle?

2 Vocabulary

Read the sentences about health and sickness and find the missing words in the word square. They are written from top to bottom, left to right, right to left and diagonally.

1 This is an _ _ _ _ _ _ _ _ _ ! Some people have been hurt in a road _ _ _ _ _ _ _ _ , and they need an _ _ _ _ _ _ _ _ _ to take them to hospital.

2 I have bad _ _ _ _ _ _ _ so the doctor sent me to the ear _ _ _ _ _ _ at the hospital. Now I have to take a _ _ _ _ three times a day to make the _ _ _ _ go away.

3 A _ _ _ _ person can't hear without the help of a hearing aid.

4 A doctor and a _ _ _ _ _ _ both work in a hospital. A _ _ _ _ _ _ _ is a sick person they look after.

5 Even if we had a _ _ _ _ to cure every disease, would everyone be _ _ _ and healthy?

6 Doctor, I feel really _ _ _ . I've got a cold, a _ _ _ _ throat, and a high temperature. And just listen to my horrible _ _ _ _ _ ! I think I've got _ _ _ .

7 When I cut myself with a bread knife, the _ _ _ _ _ was quite deep. There was a lot of blood so my face went _ _ _ _ _ , I felt _ _ _ _ _ and thought I was going to fall over, but fortunately I didn't _ _ _ _ _ .

A	M	B	U	L	A	N	C	E
C	L	I	N	I	C	U	P	M
C	S	E	H	C	A	R	A	E
I	O	Q	P	J	P	S	T	R
D	R	U	G	I	A	E	I	G
E	E	K	G	F	L	U	E	E
N	I	A	P	H	E	L	N	N
T	T	I	F	A	I	N	T	C
W	O	U	N	D	I	Z	Z	Y

57

3 Reading

Read the text and questions. For each question, decide which is the correct answer, A, B, C or D.

> I'm sure I'm not the only person my age (15) who hates going to the dentist. Channel 4's late-night documentary *Open wide* last Tuesday was excellent for people like me. However, none of my school friends watched it because they didn't know it was on. Why can't television companies let us know about such important programmes in advance?
>
> This programme was important because it showed how methods for helping people with toothache have developed over the centuries. If you think visiting the dentist today is an uncomfortable experience, just be grateful you didn't live 200 years ago! Then, the programme told us, the only cure for toothache was removing the tooth. There weren't any dentists, so the person who cut your hair also pulled out your bad teeth, and there was nothing to stop you feeling the pain.
>
> The programme has also completely changed my attitude to looking after my teeth. My parents were always saying to me things like, 'Don't eat too many sweets,' and, 'Brush your teeth after meals,' but I never paid much attention. Now I've seen what damage sugar can do, especially if I don't use a toothbrush regularly, I'm going to change my habits. Many people would benefit from a repeat of this programme.
>
> **Sophie Ashley, Oxford**

1 Why has Sophie written this letter?
A to complain about the time a television programme was shown
B to ask for more television programmes designed for school children
C to advise people to watch a particular television programme
D to persuade a television company to show a programme again

2 What can a reader find out from this letter?
A how to encourage young people to take care of their teeth
B where to get information about future television programmes
C what kinds of subjects young people enjoy studying at school
D which television channel shows the most interesting programmes

3 What did *Open wide* say about toothache?
A In the past, nobody could make it stop.
B Dentists used to help people who had it.
C Hairdressers have it more than other people.
D Ways of curing it have changed.

4 What does Sophie think about her parents now?
A They don't know as much as her about teeth.
B Their advice is worth listening to.
C They eat things which are bad for them.
D They don't clean their teeth often enough.

5 Which of these gives information about the programme Sophie watched?

A
11.30 pm *Open wide*
A play about a 19th-century dentist and how he brought comfort to his patients.

B
11.30 pm *Open wide*
The series about health care for teenagers. This week, good eating habits.

C
11.30 pm *Open wide*
This history of the dentist's profession shows what happens when we eat.

D
11.30 pm *Open wide*
How to prepare young children for that first visit to the doctor or dentist.

4 Grammar

Finish the second sentence so that it means the same as the first.

1 I took an aspirin to stop my head aching.
I took an aspirin because my ....
2 My brother goes jogging because he must keep fit.
My brother goes jogging to ....
3 If you don't give up coffee, you'll never sleep well.
You'll never sleep well unless ....
4 People with flu should stay in bed for a few days.
Stay in bed for a few days if you ....
5 Smoking isn't allowed in hospitals.
In hospitals, you can't ....

5 Writing

Write this letter to an English-speaking friend.

• You have flu and the doctor has told you to stay in bed for a few days.
• Tell your friend how you feel now, describe how you are passing the time while you are sick, and say what you plan to do when you feel better again.
• Write about 100 words.

Dear Alex,
I've got flu and I have to stay in bed until I'm better. ....
....

Get ready for PET Writing paper

1 You have 1 hour and 30 minutes for the Reading and Writing paper. The writing comes at the end of the paper so plan your time carefully.
2 There are three writing parts to the paper: completing sentences, filling in a form and writing a letter.
3 You can get 25 marks for the Writing paper: 5 marks for Part 1, 10 marks for Part 2 and 10 marks for Part 3.
4 In the exam you get a question paper and an answer sheet (see p.92-3). You can make notes on the question paper but you must write your answers on the answer sheet.

5 Write clearly. You don't want to lose marks because the examiner can't read your writing!
6 When you do Part 1, make sure that you don't make any copying mistakes.
7 You can get a lot of marks for Part 2, so do it carefully! You should only write short answers of 1–5 words.
8 When you write your letter in Part 3, make sure you follow all the instructions.
9 Near the end of the test time, check your answers.
10 There is more information about this paper in the **Get ready** boxes in this book. Make sure you read them again before the exam.

10 ① Entertainment

1 Speaking

1 How often do you do these things?

watch television	sometimes
go to the cinema	quite often
surf the Internet	not very often
go to a concert	occasionally
go to the theatre	very often
go clubbing	never

2 Match the things in this box with the different types of entertainment.

curtain	encore	website	commercial
interval	soap opera	programme	backing group
ticket	channel	soloist	chat room

3 Say what you like and dislike about each type of entertainment.

2 Vocabulary

1 Complete the text with words from the box. Use each word only once.

part	clap	reviews	rehearsal	screen	camera
performance	series	director	stage	studio	lines

An Actor speaks

As an actor, I much prefer working in the theatre to working on a film or a television **(1)** .... When I get a **(2)** .... in a play, I spend a long time learning my **(3)** .... and then there is a long period of **(4)** .... with the other actors before the first night. The good thing about a play, however, is that you are standing up on the **(5)** .... with a real live audience just a few metres away from you. At the end of the play, if they have enjoyed it, the people all **(6)** .... and you really feel good. It's interesting to read the **(7)** .... in the newspaper, but it's the people who are there who really matter. Working in film or television, however, you spend too much time waiting in the **(8)** .... while the **(9)** .... crew make all the technical arrangements. You sometimes have to do the same bit over and over again until the **(10)** .... is satisfied with your **(11)** .... Then it is months or even years before the film or programme appears on the **(12)** .... By then, you've forgotten all about it and you're in the middle of doing the next thing, anyway.

2 Choose the best answer, A, B, C, or D.

1 Why does the actor prefer working in the theatre?
A You have lots of time to practise.
B It's the same every night.
C There is a live audience.
D He always gets good reviews.

2 What does the actor dislike about working on films?

A It can be boring.

B You can get lonely.

C It is easy to forget your lines.

D You have to do two things at once.

3 **Fill in the missing word in these sentences.**

1 A .... is someone who writes in a magazine or newspaper.

2 A guitarist is someone who .... a guitar, often in a group.

4 **Make similar sentences to explain what these people do.**

drummer	director	photographer	TV presenter
disc jockey	comedian	pianist	film critic
interviewer	dancer	singer	violinist

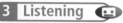 **3 Listening**

1 **Listen to two friends discussing what to do this evening. Where do they decide to go?**

A ☐   **B** ☐   **C** ☐   **D** ☐

2 **Listen to two friends talking about films. Which type of film do they decide to go and see?**

A ☐   **B** ☐   **C** ☐   **D** ☐

3 **Listen to two friends discussing a film they have each seen. What did they like most about the film?**

A the plot

B the actors

C the characters

D the camerawork

 **4 Speaking**

Talk about a film, play or TV programme you have seen recently. Say what was good and bad about it. Remember to include information about the plot, characters and actors.

5 Listening 🔊

1. You have about 30 minutes for the Listening paper.
2. There are four parts to the paper: Part 1 has seven short texts, Parts 2, 3, and 4 have one long text each.
3. You can get 25 marks for the Listening paper, one for each question.
4. There are pauses between the listening texts. Make sure you use this time to read the questions for the next part, so you are ready to answer.
5. You hear each listening text twice. Answer the questions during the first listening. Check your answers when you hear the text for the second time.
6. In the exam you get a question paper and an answer sheet (see p.92-3). As you listen, write your answers on the question paper. At the end of the test, you have extra time to copy your answers on to the answer sheet.
7. You must use pencil on the answer sheet. Take a pencil, pencil sharpener and rubber to the exam.
8. Copy your answers carefully on to the answer sheet. Mark only one letter for each question. If you make a mistake, rub it out carefully and mark the new answer clearly.
9. Listen carefully, but don't worry if there are words you don't understand. You probably don't need to know them to answer the questions.
10. If there is a question you can't answer, just leave it and move on to the next one. You will probably hear the answer the second time you listen.
11. If you don't know the answer after the two listenings, guess – you may be right!
12. There is more information about this paper in the **Get ready** boxes in this book. Make sure you read them again before the exam.

Now try this listening task. Listen twice, as in the exam.
- Look at the notes about radio programmes.
- Some information is missing.
- You will hear an announcement about the programmes.
- For each question, fill in the missing information.

THIS MORNING'S RADIO

08.00	News
	Arts Review programme
(1).......	– information about theatre, concerts and films
	– special guest: Kevin Jones, **(2)** .... in a pop band.
08.45	**(3)** .... with Graham Smith.
08.50	New series: Polly Brown talks to people about **(4)** ....
09.30	**(5)** .... with James Grant.
10.15	Radio play called **(6)** ' .... '

6 Writing

Write a letter to your English-speaking penfriend about a concert, play or film you have been to recently.
- Say where it was, who you went with, and what is was like.
- Write about 100 words.

Dear Tom,
I went to see ....
....

The age of communication

1 Speaking

1 Look at these ways of keeping in touch with people.

| letters | mobile phone | e-mail | fax | pager |

Talk about:

- how often you use each one
- what you use each one for
- the good and bad things about each one

2 Look at these two photographs. They both show people keeping in touch with their friends. Choose one of the photographs and talk about it. Remember to talk about all the things you can see, what the people are doing, and how you think they are feeling.

A

B

1 You have 10–12 minutes for the Speaking paper.
2 You take the test with another student who is your partner. There are two examiners: one tells you what to do and the other one listens. Remember to speak clearly so both examiners can hear you.
3 There are four parts to the paper: talking about yourself, a situation, a photograph, and discussing a wider theme.
4 You can get 25 marks for the Speaking paper. You get marks for how well you communicate with your partner and for your pronunciation. There are also some marks for grammar and vocabulary.
5 Listen carefully to the examiner's instructions. If you are not sure what to do, ask the examiner to repeat them.

6 In Parts 1, 2 and 4, talk to your partner – not the examiner.
7 In Parts 2 and 3 the pictures are there to help you. Talk about what you can see and don't stop after you have talked about one thing. If you can't remember the word for something, don't worry. You can describe the thing or talk about something else.
8 Try to make the test easier for your partner and the examiner by being relaxed and friendly. Remember to ask your partner questions, show an interest in what they say, and give them a chance to speak.
9 There is more information about this paper in the **Get ready** boxes in this book. Make sure you read them again before the exam.

3 Practise this Part 2 task with a friend. Remember to talk about *all* the pictures, and don't decide too soon!

The examiner says:

I'm going to describe a situation to you. A friend is going away to study in another town. She will be living on her own in a student flat. She has some money to spend on one piece of electrical equipment, but she doesn't know what to buy. Talk together about the different things she can buy, and then say which will be best.

4 In the Speaking test you have to read out your candidate number. Practise reading out these numbers:

1 61225 0143 **2** 43189 9876 **3** 90906 5539

5 You will be asked to spell a word in Part 1 of the test. Spell these things:

1 your family name
2 your first name
3 the street/district/city where you live
4 the country you come from
5 the name of the school where you study

2 Reading

Read the text below and choose the correct word, A, B, C or D, for each space.

THE RECIPE FOR GOOD COMMUNICATION

How many people do you communicate with in a day? Probably a lot more **(1)** .... you did ten years ago. With a few pieces of equipment, we can 'talk' to people in more and more ways, not **(2)** .... face-to-face and on the phone, but also via the Internet. It is very important, therefore, **(3)** .... everyone to try and improve their communication skills. Despite all the technological advances of **(4)** .... years, the art of good conversation is still at the heart of successful communication. **(5)** .... it's a good idea to remember the four golden rules of good communication. Firstly, be as clear as you can. Misunderstandings arise if we don't say exactly **(6)** .... we mean. Secondly, we have to work **(7)** .... at listening. Pay attention to what the other person is saying. Thirdly, ask **(8)** .... people what they think, don't only tell them what you think. And finally show respect for other people, give them time to say what they want, and **(9)** .... interest in what they say.

If you **(10)** .... these rules, you will be a good communicator.

1	**A** like	**B** than	**C** as	**D** that
2	**A** yet	**B** even	**C** just	**D** still
3	**A** for	**B** if	**C** by	**D** from
4	**A** close	**B** last	**C** late	**D** recent
5	**A** There	**B** So	**C** Such	**D** Or
6	**A** when	**B** what	**C** which	**D** whom
7	**A** hard	**B** much	**C** great	**D** very
8	**A** every	**B** other	**C** each	**D** another
9	**A** get	**B** put	**C** be	**D** show
10	**A** act	**B** move	**C** follow	**D** go

3 Grammar

Finish the second sentence so that it means the same as the first.

1 My parents prefer using the telephone to using e-mail.
My parents think using the telephone ....

2 My neighbour is confused by modern technology.
Modern technology ....

3 Whose is this mobile phone?
Who does ....

4 When I look at a screen for too long, I find it tiring.
When I look at a screen for too long, I get ....

5 E-mail makes contacting people a lot easier.
With e-mail, it is ....

PRACTICE TEST 1 – READING

PAPER 1 Reading and Writing Test 1 hour 30 minutes

READING

PART 1

Questions 1–5

- Look at the sign in each question.
- Someone asks you what it means.
- Mark the letter next to the correct explanation – **A, B, C or D – on your answer sheet.**

Example:

0

THESE ANIMALS ARE
DANGEROUS.
DO NOT CROSS THE
SAFETY FENCE.

A Don't get any nearer to these animals because they may hurt you.

B Don't let these animals get out from behind this fence.

C It's dangerous to bring animals into this area.

D Only cross the road with animals when it's safe to do so.

Example answer:

Part 1

0	A	B	C	D
	▬			

1

Guided tours of the cathedral tower every hour on the hour

A It takes over an hour to tour the cathedral tower.

B Meet the guide an hour before the cathedral tower tour begins.

C You'll have to wait an hour for the next tour of the cathedral tower.

D A guide shows visitors round the cathedral tower once an hour.

2

!

PASSENGERS MUST NOT CROSS THE RAILWAY LINE UNLESS WITH A MEMBER OF STAFF

A You can walk across the line if a railway worker is with you.

B Railway staff will direct passengers to the way across the line.

C Passengers are never allowed to walk across the line.

D Members of staff should prevent anyone from crossing the line.

3

The lift telephone is for use ONLY in an emergency.

A If you want to use this telephone, lift the receiver.

B Don't make ordinary calls from the lift telephone.

C All emergencies will be reported on this phone.

D Don't use the lift if there isn't an emergency .

4

PUBLIC FOOTPATH

Please shut the gate behind you

A When the gate is shut, this path isn't open to the public.

B People should walk one behind the other on this path.

C You may walk here but you shouldn't leave the gate open.

D If you want to walk here, use the gate behind you.

5

(i)

Patients with an appointment should check in at reception before entering the waiting room

A If the waiting room is full, make an appointment at reception.

B You may have to wait for your appointment, so please be patient.

C You could miss your appointment if you leave the waiting room.

D Don't go in the waiting room without informing the receptionist of your arrival.

Guided walks

A This 10-kilometre walk goes along the river valley and up into the hills, where there are wonderful views of the countryside and opportunities to watch birds as they fly south for the winter. Some paths are steep and can get muddy after rain. 8 am start; bring your own lunch.

B We leave at sunset to walk through the woods and look for birds and animals that come out after dark. Bring a torch or candle in a jar. The walk ends two hours later with refreshments in the village where the children's writer Mary Tandy has lived for many years.

C This leisurely walk (three hours) is led by a well-known local history professor. He will show you where the Romans first landed in this country, describe how the port grew in the 17th century, and take you round the historic castle.

D This short walk takes you along the beach where you can look at sea life which has been left behind in rock pools. Bring a net and container if you have them. Starting times (morning, afternoon or evening) depend on the movement of the sea. Please check in advance.

E Take an easy walk through the fields and woods of the little-known Silver River Valley, which is rich in wild flowers. Sorry, no picking! Your guide will inform you about plans to keep this area free from building development and tell you what you can do to help. Mornings only, three hours.

F Discover the wildlife and history of the coast area by walking along the cliff-top path with a knowledgeable guide. This may be done as one long walk (seven hours) or, if you prefer something less tiring, the same ground can be covered on three shorter afternoon walks.

G A fun walk with beach games, beginning at 3 pm. Look for hidden treasure among the rocks and win a prize. Children under 12 must be with a responsible adult. Walkers may also take part in the great beach clean-up. We supply rubbish bags and gloves.

H This walk is for early risers. Watch the sun come up over the hills and listen to the birds' morning song. Walk the short distance to Pirate's Cliff for a breakfast barbecue overlooking the beach. Here, stories from the past about sailors and their ships lost at sea are brought to life by local actors.

PART 2

Questions 6–10

- The people below all want to go on a guided walk.
- On the next page, there are eight descriptions of guided walks.
- Decide which walk (**letters A–H**) would be the most suitable for each person (**numbers 6–10**).
- For each of these numbers mark the correct letter **on your answer sheet.**

Example answer:

Part 2

0	A	B	C	D	E	F	G	H
	▢	▢	■	▢	▢	▢	▢	▢

6 Julia has three children under 12. They all like short walks, which always make them feel hungry and keen to stop for a snack. Julia wants to encourage the children's interest in nature and history.

7 Russell wants a morning walk which will give him the chance to find something to bring back to show his biology teacher. He has to complete some work about the seashore for her.

8 Harry likes to go on long walks along paths which less serious walkers may find difficult. He's interested in the birds and plants you can find beside rivers.

9 Marcia feels that the natural environment is in danger and likes the idea of a walk which encourages people to care for nature. She enjoys studying different varieties of wild plants.

10 Isabel is looking for a walk in the countryside she can do after studying all day. She'd like to have the opportunity to have something to eat or drink with the other walkers.

67

PART 3

Questions 11–20

- Look at the statements below about a student photography competition.
- Read the text on the next page to decide if each statement is correct or incorrect.
- If it is correct, mark **A** on your answer sheet.
- If it is not correct, mark **B** on your answer sheet.

Example answer:

Part 3

0	A	B
	▬	

11 For the competition, you should take a photograph which shows your opinion of student life.

12 The prizes for the winner include the opportunity to work for a time on a newspaper.

13 Members of the public will be able to see the winner's work.

14 There are over 100 additional prizes.

15 You can enter the competition if you are at least 14 and a student.

16 Each photographer must enter three different pictures for the competition.

17 Everyone should send an envelope with their pictures so they can be sent back.

18 You should make sure your photographs reach the judges by 1st October.

19 FEO will pay for parents to accompany winners if they are too young to travel alone.

20 Photographers will receive money for any of their pictures used in *The Daily Times*.

STUDENT PHOTOGRAPHY COMPETITION

Here's some exciting news. *The Daily Times* newspaper, together with the Further Education Organization (FEO) and The Photographers' Circle, announces a competition for young photographers.

The subject of the competition is 'modern students'. We want your pictures to tell us what it is like to be a student today. Perhaps you think students have a very comfortable life. Or you may believe they have a much harder time at college than former students had. Whatever your feelings, the judges are looking for interesting and original photographs.

The judges will be Ian Scott, the picture editor of *The Daily Times*, Pat Wilton, director of 'The Photographers' Circle, and FEO's chief executive, Christine Hall.

The first prize winner will get three days of work experience with *The Daily Times* in London, a book worth up to £50 from The Photographers' Circle, and £200 to spend on photographic equipment. *The Daily Times* will print the winning photographs in the newspaper and The Photographers' Circle will include them in an exhibition at their London gallery. The next 12 best photographers will win £100 each to spend on photographic equipment. Their pictures will also be in the FEO's calendar.

Here are the rules:

- The competition is open to students at secondary schools, and at further education, art and technical colleges in England and Wales.
- Students must be on full-time or part-time courses.
- Students must be aged 14 or over on 1st September this year.
- Three copies of each photograph should be sent in and should be no bigger than 25 x 20 cm.
- Up to five photographs may be sent in by one person.
- If photographers want their work returned, they must provide a stamped addressed envelope.
- The competition organizers will take no responsibility for lost or damaged work.
- Photographs that have already been printed in any newspaper or magazine are not acceptable.
- The final date for entries is 1st October this year. Winners will be announced in *The Daily Times* on 17th October.
- A parent or guardian must stay with any winner under the age of 18 while in London. All tickets and accommodation costs will be the responsibility of FEO.
- The judges' decisions are final.
- Photographers must agree to have their pictures printed in FEO publications and *The Daily Times* without payment. The photographer's name will be printed with any picture used in this way.

Send your photographs to:
Photography Competition, PO Box 314, London E17 6LJ.

PART 4

Questions 21–25

- Read the text and questions below.
- For each question, mark the letter next to the correct answer – **A, B, C** or **D** – on your answer sheet.

Example answer:

Part 4
0 A B C D

THE CARPENTER FAMILY

Charles and Alice Carpenter had ten daughters, two sons and numerous grandchildren and great-grandchildren. This makes the Carpenters the perfect subjects for *A Family Century*. The four-part series of programmes shows the family's story from Charles' and Alice's wedding in 1900 to a big family party in 1999.

At first, producer and director Kate O'Driscoll wanted to film a famous family, but she couldn't find a suitable one. 'The older members of famous families were really boring and couldn't remember anything about the past,' she explains. On the other hand, the four remaining Carpenter sisters are excellent storytellers with astonishing memories. The series starts tonight with Madge, Joyce, Sheila and Aline remembering their schooldays in the 1900s. Their father had a good job in the Post Office, but with such a large family there was never enough money. Madge was the only one to go to a good school, which made her look down on her sisters. She calls Joyce 'a pudding', while, in return, Joyce says Madge is 'bossy'.

The women are fascinating, funny and sad, but what makes this series so valuable is the way in which the women's experiences are shown side by side with the social and economic conditions of the day. *A Family Century* is an enjoyable slice of social history which should not be missed.

21 What is the writer trying to do in the text?

- **A** describe the problems of living in a large family
- **B** complain about people who tell boring stories
- **C** explain the importance of studying history
- **D** advise people to watch something on television

22 What can a reader learn about the Carpenter sisters from the text?

- **A** when their parents got married
- **B** how old they are now
- **C** what kind of jobs they did
- **D** how many children they had

23 Why does Madge feel she is better than her sisters?

- **A** She is the oldest.
- **B** She had the best education.
- **C** She has the clearest memory.
- **D** She has the most money.

24 What, in the writer's opinion, makes *A Family Century* valuable?

- **A** It makes you laugh and cry at the same time.
- **B** It gives ordinary people the chance to speak.
- **C** It mixes personal stories with historical fact.
- **D** It isn't afraid to tell the truth about bad times.

25 What did Kate O'Driscoll write when she first contacted the Carpenter family?

A *I'm writing a play about the lives of four sisters who grew up in the 1900s. What can you tell me about life then?*

B *We're looking for families to take part in a television game show. Can you answer questions about history correctly?*

C *I'm making a television series about the social history of the last 100 years. Could people in your family talk to us about their lives?*

D *I'd like to make a television programme about the history of your famous family. Do you have interesting memories of your schooldays?*

69

PART 5

Questions 26–35

- Read the text below and choose the correct word for each space.
- For each question, mark the letter next to the correct word – **A, B, C** or **D** – on **your answer sheet.**

Example answer:

Part 5
0 A B C D

MARY ASTELL

Mary Astell, **(0)** .... was born in 1668, was one of the first people in England to say women **(26)** .... to be educated. As a child, she was **(27)** .... clever that her uncle decided to give her lessons in French, Latin and Mathematics. In 1696, she wrote a book in which she **(28)** .... that a special college for women should be built. Some rich women **(29)** .... her idea and gave her money to start the college. However, important people in the church were against the plan and she never **(30)** .... to do what she wanted. It **(31)** .... another 200 years before the first women's college was built in Cambridge. Mary **(32)** .... on studying and writing her **(33)** .... life. If people **(34)** .... on her door when she was working, she **(35)** .... her head out of the window and said, 'Mrs Astell is not at home.' She died in 1731.

	A	B	C	D
0	who	that	what	which
26	must	ought	can	may
27	such	very	so	too
28	told	offered	suggested	informed
29	supported	agreed	helped	allowed
30	succeeded	could	arrived	managed
31	lasted	took	passed	delayed
32	went	continued	came	brought
33	whole	all	total	full
34	hit	clapped	knocked	struck
35	sent	turned	let	put

WRITING

PART 1

Questions 1–5

- Here are some sentences about some new babies.
- For each question, finish the second sentence so that it means the same as the first.
- The second sentence is started for you. **Write only the missing words on your answer sheet.**
- You may use this page for any rough work.

Example: In our family, we have two new babies.
In our family, there *are two new babies.*

1 The new babies are three months old.
   The new babies were born ....

2 The babies' names are Anna and Mark.
   The babies are ....

3 Anna drinks more milk than Mark.
   Mark doesn't drink ....

4 The babies have received many presents from friends and relations.
   Friends and relations have ....

5 Anna and Mark both sleep a lot.
   Anna sleeps a lot and so ....

PART 2

Questions 6–15

- An international magazine wants to find out about its readers' clothes-buying habits.
- You have agreed to complete the magazine's questionnaire.
- Look at the questionnaire and answer each question.
- **Write your answers on your answer sheet.**
- You may use this page for any rough work.

```
          Q U E S T I O N N A I R E

               FASHION TODAY
        27 Eastern Way, Swindon SD3 4KL, UK

Full name: (6)..........................................
Home address (including country): (7) ..............

Date of birth (day/month/year): (8) ................
Sex: (9) ...............................................
Occupation: (10) ......................................
What clothes (one thing) have you bought most recently?
(11) ...................................................
How much did it cost? (12) ...........................
How often do you buy shoes? (13) .....................
Who goes with you when you buy clothes? (14) .........
What colour do you wear most often? (15) .............

Thank you for answering our questions.
```

PART 3

Question 16

- You have just spent the evening in an English-speaking friend's house.
- Now you are writing a letter to thank this friend.
- Tell your friend what you particularly enjoyed about the evening, invite your friend to spend an evening in your home next week, and say what you plan to do then.
- **Finish the letter on your answer sheet, using about 100 words.**

Dear ......,
Thank you for the wonderful evening I had in your house. ....
....

You must write your answer on
the separate answer sheet

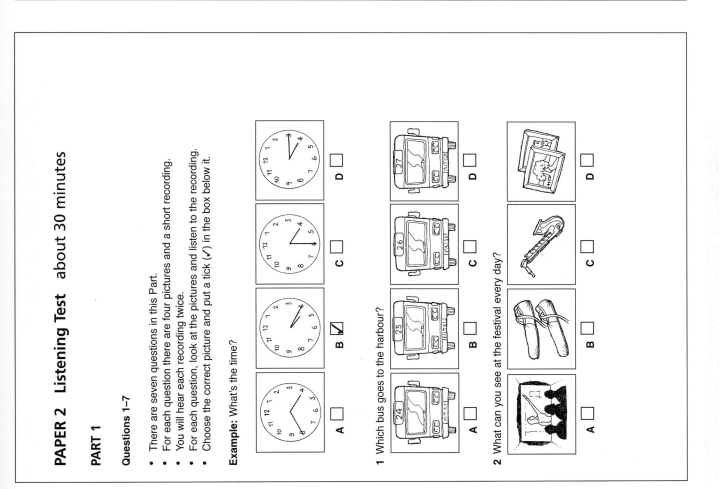

PAPER 2 Listening Test about 30 minutes

PART 1

Questions 1–7

- There are seven questions in this Part.
- For each question there are four pictures and a short recording.
- You will hear each recording twice.
- For each question, look at the pictures and listen to the recording.
- Choose the correct picture and put a tick (✓) in the box below it.

Example: What's the time?

A ☐   B ☑   C ☐   D ☐

1 Which bus goes to the harbour?

A ☐   B ☐   C ☐   D ☐

2 What can you see at the festival every day?

A ☐   B ☐   C ☐   D ☐

3 Where does the boy find his keys?

A ☐   B ☐   C ☐   D ☐

4 What present are they going to buy?

A ☐   B ☐   C ☐   D ☐

5 What is today's soup made from?

A ☐   B ☐   C ☐   D ☐

6 Which instrument is Lucy playing these days?

A ☐   B ☐   C ☐   D ☐

7 How will John travel to London?

A ☐   B ☐   C ☐   D ☐

PART 2

Questions 8–13

- Look at the questions for this Part.
- You will hear a woman talking about her work.
- Put a tick (✔) in the correct box for each question.

8   In her first job, Kathy worked as

A   an economist.
B   a salesperson.
C   a flight attendant.
D   a travel agent.

9   Why did Kathy first go to China?

A   on holiday
B   to start a business
C   as part of her job
D   to buy some things

10   What problem did Kathy have on her second trip to China?

A   She had too little money to buy the silk.
B   She couldn't find the people who sold the silk.
C   She wasn't able to buy a small amount of silk.
D   She had problems transporting the silk.

11   When Kathy started her business in London

A   she only made shirts.
B   she worked in her own home.
C   she continued working for the airline.
D   she made all the clothes herself.

12   Why are Kathy's clothes so popular?

A   They are all made in China.
B   They are all made out of silk.
C   They are not like other clothes.
D   They are designed for famous people.

13   How is Kathy's business changing?

A   She doesn't only make clothes these days.
B   She is not using Chinese silk anymore.
C   She is making clothes out of cheaper materials.
D   She doesn't design the clothes herself anymore.

PART 3

Questions 14–19

- Look at the information about a holiday in Australia.
- Some information is missing.
- You will hear a man talking about his holiday.
- For each question, fill in the missing information in the numbered spaces.

HOLIDAY IN AUSTRALIA

Name of the island: (14) ....
Best way to get there: By (15) ....
Number of rooms in the hotel: (16) ....

Activities available at the Kids' Club:
- collecting shells
- (17) ....
- watersports
- concert for parents

Activities available to all visitors:
- (18) ....
- deep-sea diving
- studying local wildlife

Things to buy on the island:
- work by local (19) ....
- T-shirts and baseball caps

PART 4

Questions 20–25

- Look at the six statements for this Part.
- You will hear a conversation between two teenage friends, Tom, a boy, and Sally, a girl.
- Decide if you think each statement is correct or incorrect.
- If you think it is correct, put a tick (✓) in the box under **A** for **YES**. If you think it is incorrect, put a tick in the box under **B** for **NO**.

		A YES	B NO
20	Tom finds his mother's attitude difficult to understand.	☐	☐
21	Sally thinks that Tom's mother is being unfair.	☐	☐
22	Tom agrees that his car-cleaning business was unsuccessful.	☐	☐
23	Tom thinks that parents will pay to see the show.	☐	☐
24	Sally is unsure whether the show is a good idea or not.	☐	☐
25	Sally agrees to take part in the show.	☐	☐

PAPER 3 Speaking Test about 12 minutes

PART 1 (2–3 minutes)

Before the test begins the examiner asks you to read out your candidate number.
In this part of the test you will have to ask your partner questions about personal details,
for example, where he or she lives, goes to school or work, etc. You also have to answer
your partner's questions.
At the end of Part 1 the examiner will ask you to spell a word, for example part of your
name, address etc.

PART 2 (2–3 minutes)

The examiner says:

I'm going to describe a situation to you.
One of the students in your class is leaving to go and live abroad with his/her family.
You would like to give him/her a present on the last day of school. Talk together about
the sorts of presents you can give and then decide which will be best. (See p.77.)

PART 3 (3 minutes)

The examiner says:

Now I'm going to give each of you a photograph of people relaxing. Would you show
it to your partner and talk about it please. (See p.78.)

PART 4 (3 minutes)

The examiner says:

Your photographs both showed people relaxing. Now I'd like you to talk together
about what you do when you want to relax, when you are alone and when you are
with friends.

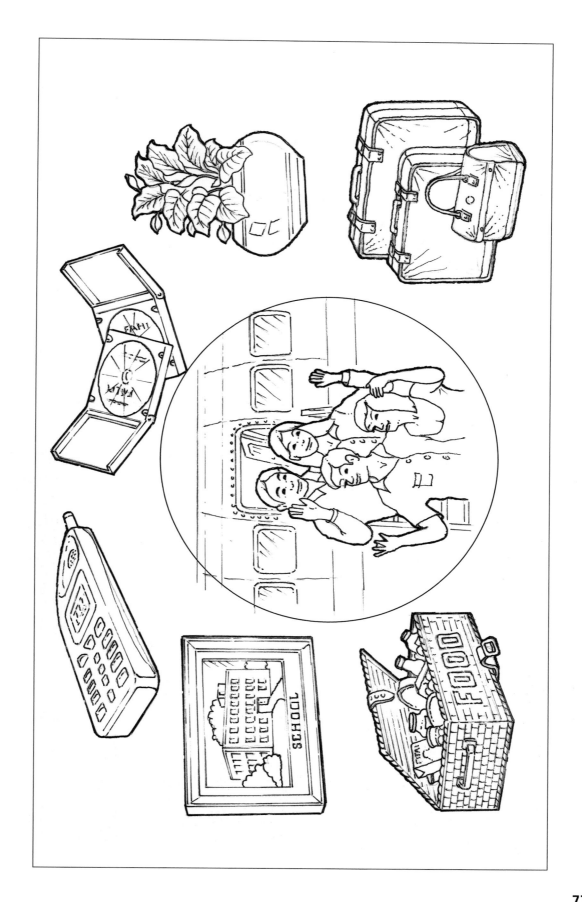

PAPER 1 Reading and Writing Test 1 hour 30 minutes

READING

PART 1

Questions 1–5

- Look at the sign in each question.
- Someone asks you what it means.
- Mark the letter next to the correct explanation – **A, B, C or D – on your answer sheet.**

Example:

0

THESE ANIMALS ARE
DANGEROUS.
DO NOT CROSS THE
SAFETY FENCE.

A Don't get any nearer to these animals
 because they may hurt you.
B Don't let these animals get out from
 behind this fence.
C It's dangerous to bring animals into this
 area.
D Only cross the road with animals when
 it's safe to do so.

Example answer:

Part 1

0 A B C D

1

Offer this seat to old or
disabled people, or those
carrying young children.

A Young children should offer their seats
 to anyone older than them.
B If you have children with you, don't let
 them sit on this seat.
C This seat is mainly for people who find it
 difficult to stand.
D Help disabled people by offering to carry
 their children for them.

2

PLEASE KEEP YOUR
PERSONAL PROPERTY
AND CLOTHING CLEAR OF
THE LIFT DOORS.

A Make sure your things aren't in the way
 of the lift doors.
B You must wear proper clothes if you
 want to come in here.
C Don't use this lift for transporting your
 personal belongings.
D Don't leave any of your things behind
 when you get out of the lift.

3

*We cannot allow
latecomers to enter
until a suitable
break in the play.*

A We'll start late so there won't be a
 break in the play.
B There's a break in the play when you
 can leave if you want to.
C Some people watching this play may not
 find it suitable.
D If you're late, you won't be able to go in
 immediately.

4

ANY BICYCLE LEFT HERE
FOR MORE THAN 14 DAYS
WILL BE REMOVED.

A You can't park your bicycle here for
 longer than two weeks.
B We are holding a sale of bicycles here
 for the next 14 days.
C For two weeks from today, bicycles
 should keep to the left on this road.
D This bicycle park will be closed for
 14 days.

5

SPORTS CENTRE

Sorry! Gym showers
out of order.
Use ones by swimming pool.

A We're sorry none of the showers in the
 sports centre is working.
B After using the gym, you'll have to go
 somewhere else for a shower.
C The showers are better in the gym than
 in the swimming pool.
D Book your shower before you use the
 gym or swimming pool.

PRACTICE TEST 2 – READING

PART 2

Questions 6–10

- The people below all want to buy a CD-ROM.
- On the next page there are descriptions of eight CD-ROMs.
- Decide which CD-ROM (letters **A–H**) would be the most suitable for each person (numbers **6–10**).
- For each of these numbers, mark the correct letter **on your answer sheet.**

Example answer:

Part 2

0	A	B	C	D	E	F	G	H
	▬							

6 Gerry would like to help his 16-year-old daughter who has always dreamt of flying planes. She can't be a pilot because of her eyesight, and he wants her to think about other job possibilities.

7 Erica is looking for a present for her 14-year-old son. He loves planes. He wants something which will start playing music himself.

8 Paula knows she has a good figure but apart from that she isn't satisfied with the way she looks. She wants something which will help her change her appearance.

9 Daniel got some money for his thirteenth birthday from his grandmother. He really wants to get a racing game, but she says he must buy something which will help him with his school work.

10 Patricia (15) loves speed and even writes poems about it. She can't wait to have driving lessons and would like something which gives her a good idea about being in control of any kind of vehicle.

CD-ROMs

A Magic makeover

Have you ever wanted to see whether a new hairstyle would suit you before you visit the hairdresser's? Now you can experiment with hundreds of hairstyles, glasses and make-up fashions. Both men and women can find the perfect face for themselves with this useful tool.

B Write now

Young people (aged 8–18) can develop their writing skills, creativity and story-telling ability by writing about a very important subject: themselves. They are encouraged to write poems, songs, diaries and stories about their family and friends, things they love and hate, their secret hopes and wishes.

C Take off

This is more than just a game because you really learn how to fly a plane or helicopter. You study a detailed instruction guide and practise on screen with sets of flight instruments from a variety of aircraft. Experience taking off and landing at any one of 3,000 airports worldwide.

D Speedkid

Young people aged 3–15 can explore and discover with these educational games. Difficulty levels can be changed to suit any player. Activities range from maths problems to word games, from drawing to language learning, all based around fun with fast cars, high-speed trains and planes.

E Top notes

This is an enormous library of all types of music from the last 80 years. Watch performances, listen to recordings, look at 9,000 album covers and photos, and read articles on 4,000 artists. You can search by artist's name, type of music, or period.

F Choose right

This is an essential guide to making the right career decision. You complete a detailed questionnaire and it tells you what you're good at, including your social, practical, creative and leadership strengths. It then shows you what further education and career choices are open to you.

G Personal trainer

You tell the 'trainer' details about your weight, height, etc, and it will give you a personal fitness and body-shaping programme. Whether you are male or female, young or old, want something difficult or easy, you will find a series of suitable exercises here which will make you look and feel better.

H Master class

This has 50 hours of instruction and will give you the basic skills needed to play the guitar. All beginners can learn to play their favourite songs. You can practise in private, but very soon you'll be confident enough to perform in public. You could even make it your career!

★★★★★ WHISTLER, WESTERN CANADA ★★★★★
Where standards are higher, and so are the mountains!

In the spectacular Coast Mountains of British Columbia, just 120 km north of Vancouver and the coast, lies the beautiful village of Whistler.

Winter sports

The country round Whistler is considered by many to be the number one ski resort in North America for a number of reasons:

★ It has the largest skiing area on the continent, with more than 200 marked tracks.

★ It has the two steepest skiing mountains in North America: Blackcomb and Whistler.

★ There are five separate mountain bases, all within five minutes of each other and all with high-speed lifts. This means skiers can reach the ski slopes quickly without ever having to queue for a lift.

★ Visitors have the convenience of being able to ski directly to and from their accommodation in Whistler Village.

★ The winter season runs from November to May, with summer skiing and snowboarding continuing until August.

★ There is an average annual snowfall of 9 m, plus snow-making systems.

★ Additional winter activities include ice-skating, snow-shoeing, paragliding and snowmobiling.

Whistler village

After an exciting day on the slopes, visitors can explore this lovely pedestrian-only village. There are many interesting shops and boutiques, and a variety of places for a drink and a snack, or a delicious meal. Those who are still not tired can dance the night away in a nightclub before going back to rest in one of Whistler's many comfortable hotels and inns. There is a choice of accommodation in all price ranges, though most of it is at the top end of the range.

Summer time

Whistler, the number one ski resort in North America, shows how enjoyable summer in the mountains can be.

With four world-class golf courses, Whistler has become popular as a golfing destination. Each course tests the player's skill in a different way, but all have amazing views. The Whistler Golf Club was given a silver medal for its service by *Golf Magazine*. And remember, it may be summer, but it's still the skiing season in Whistler, so you can ski in the morning and have a game of golf in the afternoon.

The view from the top of either Blackcomb or Whistler mountains will take your breath away. You can go on a guided nature walk, or just go up in the lift to enjoy mountaintop dining. Other unforgettable experiences are a horseback ride above the clouds, or, for the adventurous, a high-speed guided bike ride down the mountain.

There are five lakes and numerous rivers in the Whistler valley, so the visitor has many opportunities to fish, swim, windsurf, canoe, or just relax in the sun on a warm, sandy beach.

PART 3

Questions 11–20

- Look at the statements below about Whistler in Western Canada.
- Read the text on the next page to decide if each statement is correct or incorrect.
- If it is correct, mark **A** on your answer sheet.
- If it is not correct, mark **B** on your answer sheet.

Example answer:

Part 3		
0	A	B
	▬	☐

11 The distance between Whistler and the sea is less than 150 km.

12 The Whistler area is attractive to skiers because there are many steep tracks.

13 Skiers may have to wait five minutes for their turn on a lift.

14 Skiers should take off their skis before entering Whistler village.

15 Plenty of snow falls naturally each year but, if necessary, nature can be helped.

16 You have to go from place to place in Whistler village on foot.

17 There are more cheap hotels than expensive ones in Whistler village.

18 In summer, it's possible to go skiing and play golf on the same day.

19 A guide will show you the best way to cycle to the top of the mountain.

20 In the mountains, it's too cold to sunbathe or swim in the lakes.

PART 4

Questions 21–25

- Read the text and questions below.
- For each question, mark the letter next to the correct answer – **A, B, C** or **D** – on your answer sheet.

Example answer:

Part 4
0 A **B** C D
▬ ▭ ▭ ▭

Tania Moffat, 21, works in her parents' clothes shop with her 18-year-old brother, Rufus. This is what she says:

As children, we used to fight a lot. Rufus did things like steal my diary and read out bits at dinner, but now we've put our childhood differences behind us. Of course, we still argue but these days, because we share an interest in fashion and have common aims for the business, our arguments are positive. Rufus and I manage the shop, while our parents design the clothes we sell. We are often photographed wearing the clothes. Rufus loves to wear things that are unusual or shocking and people come into the shop just to see what he's got on that day. He could become a model in the future.

Our parents got married and had me when they were still teenagers and have brought us up in a free way. When I was a schoolgirl, they often suggested I forgot about my homework and went out instead. When I decided to leave school at 16 and come and work in the shop, they supported me. They knew I had a lot to offer the company, and now they say they couldn't manage without Rufus and me. Their attitude means we all enjoy ourselves, both at home and at work.

21 What is Tania trying to do in this text?

- **A** recommend a good place to buy clothes
- **B** show people how to start their own company
- **C** describe what it's like working in her family's business
- **D** encourage young people to leave school and start work

22 What can a reader find out from this text?

- **A** Tania's attitude to marriage
- **B** Tania's opinion of today's fashions
- **C** Tania's ideas about her future
- **D** Tania's feelings about her job

23 What does Tania's father do?

- **A** He's a fashion designer.
- **B** He's a photographer.
- **C** He's manager of a shop.
- **D** He's a model.

24 What does Tania think about her brother?

- **A** He does things just to make her angry.
- **B** He's easier to get on with than before.
- **C** He isn't as serious about his work as her.
- **D** He should pay more attention to his clothes.

25 What would be the best title for this text?

- **A** *How to avoid arguing with your parents*
- **B** *Why working with your brother is a mistake*
- **C** *Successful and happy at work at only 21*
- **D** *The secret diary of a shop assistant*

PART 5

Questions 26–35

- Read the text below and choose the correct word for each space.
- For each question, mark the letter next to the correct word – **A**, **B**, **C** or **D** – on your answer sheet.

Example answer:

Part 5
0	**A**	**B**	**C**	**D**
	▬	☐	☐	☐

TRAVEL SICKNESS

Everyone loves to **(0)** .... different places and for most of us the journey between places is also exciting. But **(26)** .... people hate travelling in any kind of vehicle because it **(27)** .... them ill. It happens most often when travelling in cars along roads **(28)** .... go up and down a lot or have many bends, or on boats when the sea is **(29)** .... With travel sickness, people feel dizzy and sick and may **(30)** .... their balance, but they usually feel better as **(31)** .... as the vehicle stops moving and they can **(32)** .... out on to firm ground. The **(33)** .... of the sickness is a small problem in the ear. There are pills you can take to **(34)** .... the sickness, but you **(35)** .... to be careful because after taking these you sometimes feel sleepy.

0	**A** visit	**B** look	**C** stay	**D** drive
26	**A** another	**B** any	**C** some	**D** one
27	**A** does	**B** puts	**C** turns	**D** makes
28	**A** which	**B** who	**C** what	**D** whose
29	**A** hard	**B** rough	**C** sharp	**D** strong
30	**A** drop	**B** lose	**C** forget	**D** fail
31	**A** often	**B** well	**C** soon	**D** quickly
32	**A** step	**B** leave	**C** depart	**D** change
33	**A** reason	**B** purpose	**C** cause	**D** birth
34	**A** defend	**B** pass	**C** mend	**D** prevent
35	**A** should	**B** must	**C** will	**D** have

WRITING

PART 1

Questions 1–5

- Here are some sentences about a visit to the zoo.
- For each question, finish the second sentence so that it means the same as the first.
- The second sentence is started for you. **Write only the missing words on your answer sheet.**
- You may use this page for any rough work.

Example: Shall we go to the zoo today?
What about *going to the zoo today?*

1 The tickets to the zoo aren't expensive.
   The tickets to the zoo don't ....

2 Richard asked to visit the lions first.
   Richard said, 'Can ....

3 You mustn't give food to the animals.
   Giving food to the animals ....

4 In this zoo, there are only a few elephants.
   In this zoo, there aren't ....

5 This monkey likes talking to people.
   This is the monkey which ....

PART 2

Questions 6–15

- You would like to have a penfriend you can write to in English.
- A penfriend agency has sent you an application form to fill in.
- Look at the form and answer each question.
- **Write your answers on your answer sheet.**
- You may use this page for any rough work.

> INTERNATIONAL PENFRIENDS AGENCY
> 16 Linden Avenue, Nottingham NG6 5TH, UK
>
> ### Application form
>
> Full name: **(6)** ....
> Home address (including country): **(7)** ....
> ....
> Nationality: **(8)** ....
> Age last birthday: **(9)** ....
> Job (if you are a student, say what subjects you study): **(10)** ....
> ....
> Hobbies and free-time interests: **(11)** ....
> How often will you be able to write to your penfriend?
> **(12)** ....
> Which country would you like your penfriend to come from?
> **(13)** ....
> How did you hear about our agency? **(14)** ....
> Signature: **(15)** ....

PART 3

Question 16

- In your last English lesson, a new teacher taught the class.
- Now you are writing a letter to an English-speaking friend.
- Describe the new teacher, explain what happened in the class, and say how the students felt about it.
- **Finish the letter on your answer sheet, using about 100 words.**

Dear · · · · · ·,
I want to tell you about my new English teacher. ....
....

You must write your answer on
the separate answer sheet

PAPER 2   Listening Test   about 30 minutes

PART 1

Questions 1–7

- There are seven questions in this Part.
- For each question there are four pictures and a short recording.
- You will hear each recording twice.
- For each question, look at the pictures and listen to the recording.
- Choose the correct picture and put a tick (✓) in the box below it.

Example: What's the time?

A □   B ☑   C □   D □

1 What did the boy have for lunch today?

A □   B □   C □   D □

2 Which programme will they watch on television?

A □   B □   C □   D □

3 What time will the flight to Pisa leave?

A □   B □   C □   D □

4 Which activity did the girl do most of the time?

A □   B □   C □   D □

5 Which is the missing handbag?

A □   B □   C □   D □

6 How will they travel this weekend?

A □   B □   C □   D □

7 Which T-shirt do they decide to buy Sarah?

A □   B □   C □   D □

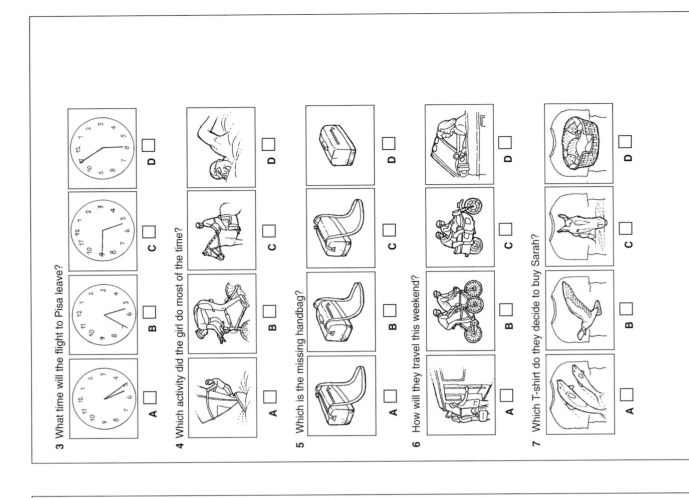

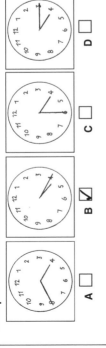

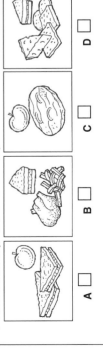

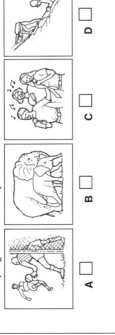

PART 2

Questions 8–13

- Look at the questions for this Part.
- You will hear a woman talking about courses at a college.
- Put a tick (✔) in the correct box for each question.

8 A course at the college is suitable for people who

- A ☐ need to study to get a job.
- B ☐ have to pass an examination.
- C ☐ are below a certain age.
- D ☐ want to have fun studying.

9 If you decide to do a course, you have to pay

- A ☐ for each lesson separately.
- B ☐ on a monthly basis.
- C ☐ the whole fee in advance.
- D ☐ a deposit before the first lesson.

10 Which language can you study for the first time this year?

- A ☐ French
- B ☐ Russian
- C ☐ German
- D ☐ Italian

11 Which cookery course is new this year?

- A ☐ basic kitchen skills
- B ☐ advanced cake-making
- C ☐ cooking for special occasions
- D ☐ vegetarian cooking

12 Why can't the college run a course about making pots?

- A ☐ There isn't enough space.
- B ☐ None of the staff can teach it.
- C ☐ They don't have the right equipment.
- D ☐ Not enough people are interested.

13 The new painting course will take place

- A ☐ two days a week.
- B ☐ every day for two weeks.
- C ☐ two afternoons a month.
- D ☐ for two months only.

PART 3

Questions 14–19

- Look at the notes about an artist.
- Some information is missing.
- You will hear the artist talking about his work.
- For each question, fill in the missing information in the numbered space.

PAUL HUNTER: ARTIST

Paul first became interested in drawing when he was **(14)** .... years old.

Paul's first wildlife drawings were of **(15)** .... he saw in the garden.

As a student, Paul did paintings of animals such as **(16)** .... to make money.

The first exhibition of Paul's work was held in a shop which used to sell **(17)** ....

Paul says that his father was a very good **(18)** .... at the exhibition.

People like Paul's paintings because the animals he paints look **(19)** ....

PART 4

Questions 20–25

- Look at the six statements for this Part.
- You will hear a conversation between two teenage friends, Jon, a boy, and Clare, a girl.
- Decide if you think each statement is correct or incorrect.
- If you think it is correct, put a tick (✓) in the box under **A** for **YES**. If you think it is incorrect, put a tick in the box under **B** for **NO**.

		A **YES**	**B** **NO**
20	This was Clare's first holiday in another country.	☐	☐
21	Clare had to understand a foreign language on holiday.	☐	☐
22	Clare enjoyed the lunches she ate on holiday.	☐	☐
23	Jon likes trying foreign food when he's on holiday.	☐	☐
24	Jon thinks Clare's father was right to make her try new things.	☐	☐
25	Clare thinks the last meal of her holiday was the best one.	☐	☐

PAPER 3   Speaking Test   about 12 minutes

PART 1 (2–3 minutes)

Before the test begins the examiner asks you to read out your candidate number.
In this part of the test you will have to ask your partner questions about personal details, for example, where he or she lives, goes to school or work, etc. You also have to answer your partner's questions.
At the end of Part 1 the examiner will ask you to spell a word, for example part of your name, address etc.

PART 2 (2–3 minutes)

The examiner says:

I'm going to describe a situation to you.
A family with young children wants to buy an animal to keep as a pet. Talk together about the types of animals which make good pets and decide which will be best for a family with young children. (See p.90.)

PART 3 (3 minutes)

The examiner says:

Now I'm going to give each of you a photograph of people enjoying themselves.
Would you show it to your partner and talk about it please. (See p.91.)

PART 4 (3 minutes)

The examiner says:

Your photographs both showed people enjoying themselves. Now I'd like you to talk together about what you do when you want to enjoy yourself, when you are at home and when you are on holiday.

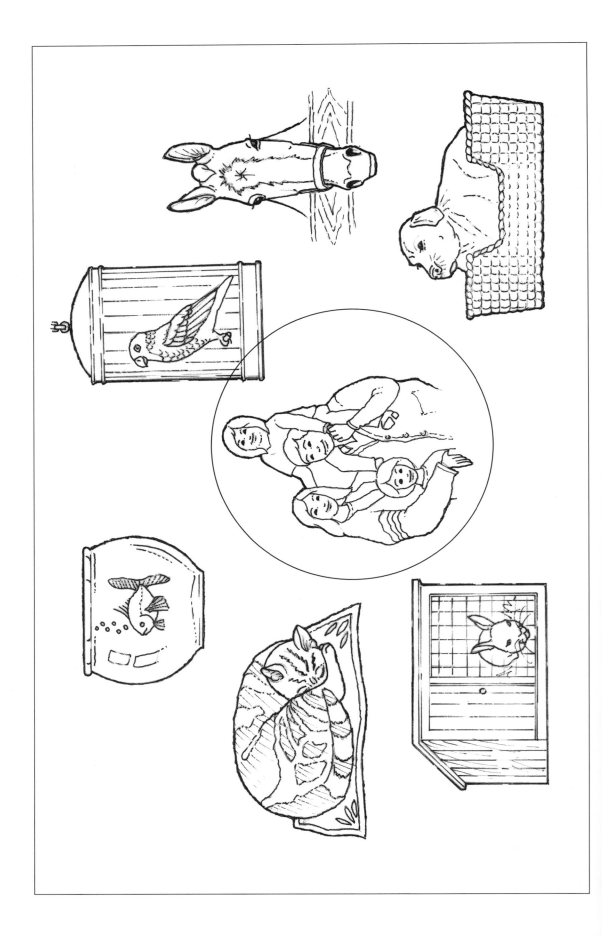

READING AND WRITING – ANSWER SHEET 1

UNIVERSITY of CAMBRIDGE
Local Examinations Syndicate

Candidate Name
If not already printed, write name
in CAPITALS and complete the
Candidate No. grid (in pencil).

Candidate's signature

Examination Title

Centre

Supervisor:
☒ If the candidate is ABSENT or has WITHDRAWN shade here ▭

Centre No.

Candidate No.

**Examination
Details**

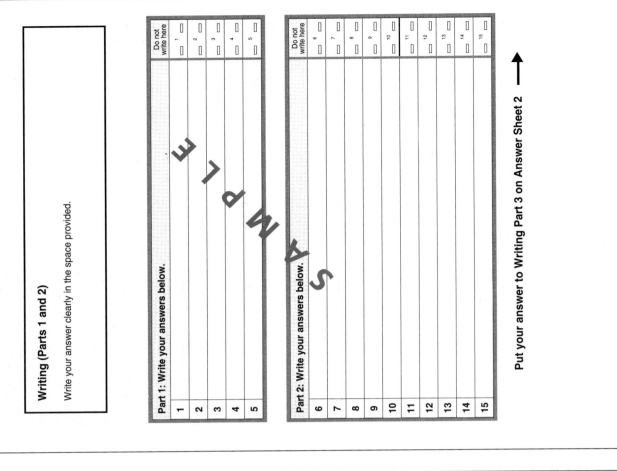

PET Reading and Writing Answer Sheet 1

Reading

Use a pencil.

Mark one letter for each question.

Example:
If you think A is the right answer to the question,
mark your answer sheet like this:

0 A̲ B C D

Rub out any answer you want to change, with an eraser.

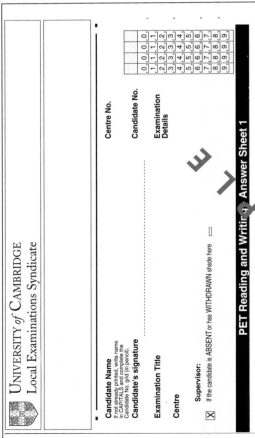

Part 1	
1	A B C D
2	A B C D
3	A B C D
4	A B C D
5	A B C D

Part 2	
6	A B C D E F G H
7	A B C D E F G H
8	A B C D E F G H
9	A B C D E F G H
10	A B C D E F G H

Part 3	
11	A B
12	A B
13	A B
14	A B
15	A B
16	A B
17	A B
18	A B
19	A B
20	A B

Part 4	
21	A B C D
22	A B C D
23	A B C D
24	A B C D
25	A B C D

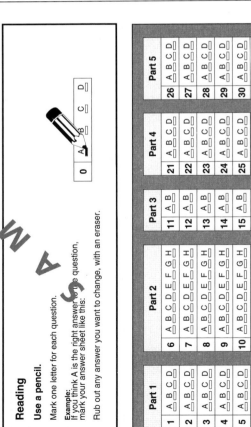

Part 5	
26	A B C D
27	A B C D
28	A B C D
29	A B C D
30	A B C D
31	A B C D
32	A B C D
33	A B C D
34	A B C D
35	A B C D

Continue on the other side of this sheet →

READING AND WRITING – ANSWER SHEET 1 (REVERSE)

Writing (Parts 1 and 2)

Write your answer clearly in the space provided.

SAMPLE

Part 1: Write your answers below.

		Do not write here
1		1
2		2
3		3
4		4
5		5

Part 2: Write your answers below.

		Do not write here
6		6
7		7
8		8
9		9
10		10
11		11
12		12
13		13
14		14
15		15

Put your answer to Writing Part 3 on Answer Sheet 2 →

LISTENING – ANSWER SHEET

UNIVERSITY of CAMBRIDGE
Local Examinations Syndicate

Candidate Name
If not already printed, write name
in CAPITALS and complete the
Candidate No. grid (in pencil).

Candidate's signature

Examination Title

Centre

Supervisor:
☒ If the candidate is ABSENT or has WITHDRAWN shade here ☐

Centre No.

Candidate No.

Examination
Details

SAMPLE

PET Listening Answer Sheet

• You must transfer all your answers from the Listening Question Paper to this answer sheet.

Use a pencil

For Parts 1,2 and 4: Mark one letter for each question.

For example, if you think A is the right answer to
the question, mark your answer sheet like this:

| 0 | A B C D |

For Part 3: Write your answers in the spaces
next to the numbers (14 - 19) like this:

| 0 | example |

Change your answer
like this:

| 0 | example |

Part 1		Part 2		Part 3	Do not write here	Part 4
1	A B C D	8	A B C D	14	14	20	A B
2	A B C D	9	A B C D	15	15	21	A B
3	A B C D	10	A B C D	16	16	22	A B
4	A B C D	11	A B C D	17	17	23	A B
5	A B C D	12	A B C D	18	18	24	A B
6	A B C D	13	A B C D	19	19	25	A B
7	A B C D						

© UCLES – EFL

READING AND WRITING – ANSWER SHEET 2

Part 3: Write your answer in the box below.

SAMPLE

Do not write below this line

This section for use by SECOND Examiner only

Marks:

Task	0	1	2	3	4	5

Language	0	1	2	3	4	5

Examiner Number

| 0 1 2 3 4 5 6 7 8 9 |
| 0 1 2 3 4 5 6 7 8 9 |
| 0 1 2 3 4 5 6 7 8 9 |
| 0 1 2 3 4 5 6 7 8 9 |

© UCLES – EFL

93

Irregular verbs

present	past simple	past perfect
be	was/were	been
beat	beat	beaten
become	became	become
begin	began	begun
bend	bent	bent
bite	bit	bitten
bleed	bled	bled
blow	blew	blown
break	broke	broken
bring	brought	brought
build	built	built
burn	burnt	burnt
buy	bought	bought
catch	caught	caught
choose	chose	chosen
come	came	come
cost	cost	cost
cut	cut	cut
dig	dug	dug
do	did	done
draw	drew	drawn
dream	dreamt	dreamt
drink	drank	drunk
drive	drove	driven
eat	ate	eaten
fall	fell	fallen
feed	fed	fed
feel	felt	felt
fight	fought	fought
find	found	found
fly	flew	flown
forget	forgot	forgotten
forgive	forgave	forgiven
freeze	froze	frozen
get	got	got
give	gave	given
go	went	gone
grow	grew	grown
have	had	had
hear	heard	heard
hide	hid	hidden
hit	hit	hit
hold	held	held
hurt	hurt	hurt
keep	kept	kept
know	knew	known
lay	laid	laid
lead	led	led

present	past simple	past perfect
learn	learnt	learnt
leave	left	left
lend	lent	lent
let	let	let
lie	lay	lain
light	lit	lit
lose	lost	lost
make	made	made
mean	meant	meant
meet	met	met
pay	paid	paid
put	put	put
read	read	read
ride	rode	ridden
ring	rang	rung
rise	rose	risen
run	ran	run
say	said	said
see	saw	seen
sell	sold	sold
send	sent	sent
set	set	set
shake	shook	shaken
shine	shone	shone
shoot	shot	shot
show	showed	shown
shut	shut	shut
sing	sang	sung
sit	sat	sat
sleep	slept	slept
smell	smelt	smelt
speak	spoke	spoken
spell	spelt	spelt
spend	spent	spent
spread	spread	spread
stand	stood	stood
steal	stole	stolen
sweep	swept	swept
swim	swam	swum
take	took	taken
teach	taught	taught
tear	tore	torn
tell	told	told
think	thought	thought
throw	threw	thrown
wake	woke	woken
wear	wore	worn
win	won	won
write	wrote	written